THE RUSSIAN SCIENTIST

THE RUSSIAN SCIENTIST

Albert Parry

RUSSIA OLD AND NEW SERIES
Jules Koslow, General Editor

The Macmillan Company, New York, New York
Collier-Macmillan Ltd., London

The Macmillan Company
866 Third Avenue, New York, N.Y. 10022
Collier-Macmillan Canada Ltd., Toronto, Ontario

Library of Congress Catalog Card Number: 72–92454
FIRST PRINTING

Printed in the United States of America

Contents

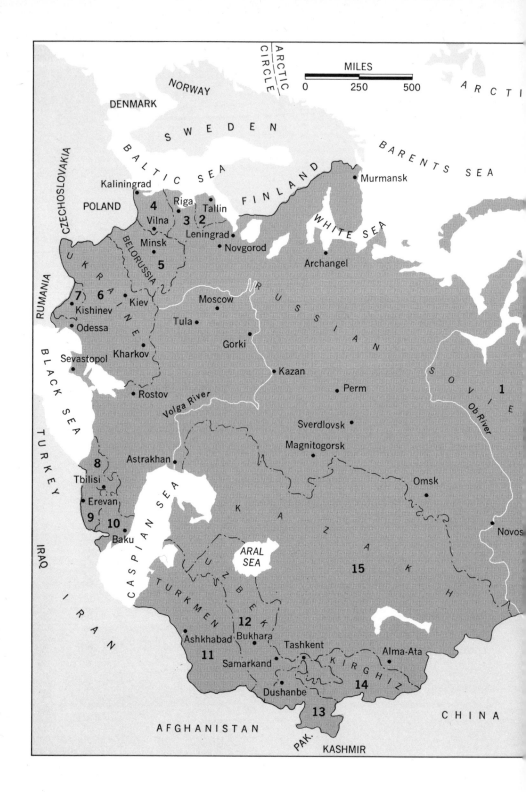

ARCTIC CIRCLE

MILES
0   250   500

ARCTI

NORWAY

DENMARK

SWEDEN

BALTIC SEA

BARENTS SEA

FINLAND

Murmansk

CZECHOSLOVAKIA

Kaliningrad

POLAND

4 Riga
Vilna 3 2 Tallin
Leningrad
Minsk
Novgorod

BELORUSSIA

5

WHITE SEA

Archangel

RUMANIA

UKRAINE

7 6 Kiev
Kishinev
Odessa

Moscow

Tula

Gorki

RUSSIAN

SOVIE

1

Ob River

Kharkov
Sevastopol

Kazan

Perm

Rostov

Volga River

Sverdlovsk

Magnitogorsk

BLACK SEA

TURKEY

8
Tbilisi
Erevan
9 10
Baku

Astrakhan

CASPIAN SEA

KAZAK

Omsk

Novos

IRAQ

IRAN

TURKMEN

UZBEK

ARAL SEA

15

12
Ashkhabad Bukhara
11 Samarkand
Dushanbe

Tashkent

KIRGHIZ

Alma-Ata

14

13

AFGHANISTAN

PAK.

KASHMIR

CHINA

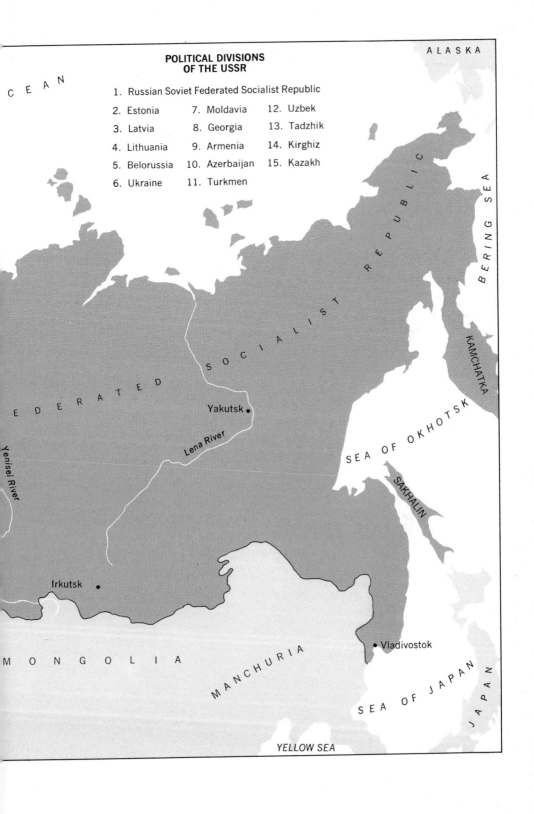

**POLITICAL DIVISIONS
OF THE USSR**

1. Russian Soviet Federated Socialist Republic

2. Estonia	7. Moldavia	12. Uzbek
3. Latvia	8. Georgia	13. Tadzhik
4. Lithuania	9. Armenia	14. Kirghiz
5. Belorussia	10. Azerbaijan	15. Kazakh
6. Ukraine	11. Turkmen	

ALASKA

C E A N

BERING SEA

KAMCHATKA

SOCIALIST REPUBLIC

EDERATED

Yenisei River

Yakutsk

Lena River

SEA OF OKHOTSK

SAKHALIN

Irkutsk

Vladivostok

MONGOLIA

MANCHURIA

SEA OF JAPAN

JAPAN

YELLOW SEA

Introduction

THE periodic table of elements? Yes, indeed, most American high school and college students know about it. But few know that a nineteenth-century Russian chemist was the table's originator. Still fewer know his name—Dmitry Mendeleyev.

Only a handful of ordinary citizens in the West may recognize the name of Ivan Pavlov. At that, you have to add, "Experiments with dogs. Remember?" "Ah yes," the answer may come. "The Russian who proved that dogs have conditioned reflexes."

In the West, people both young and old are not too aware of what the East has contributed to the world's science and technology. Some recall that it was the ancient Chinese who first invented gunpowder and printing, that the medieval Arabs were good in algebra, and that in modern times it was the Russians who were so clever about sputniks and other rocketry. But while the man in the Western street may know something about Russia's literature or music, he knows little or nothing about her science.

The names of such writers as Feodor Dostoevsky or Leo Tolstoy or Anton Chekhov are familiar to many in the West. Even the

The sputnik launches of 1957–58 alerted the West to
Russia's scientific advancements. Shown here is Sputnik
III on display in Moscow. *Sovfoto*

latter-day Boris Pasternak is remembered for his novel *Doctor Zhivago*, though more because the book was made into a popular American film with a catchy tune than because of any wide Western readership and recall of the book itself. More recently, the worldwide fame of Alexander Solzhenitsyn has extended to North America mainly because of the publicity brought to him by his Nobel Prize, but English translations of his novels are used more as coffee-table exhibits than for actual reading.

Russia's musical scores and tunes by Peter Tchaikovsky, Modest Moussorgsky, Nikolai Rimsky-Korsakov, and others are heard, liked, and remembered in the West, along with the names and even bits of biographies of some of these Slavic composers.

But Russian science? Even when the first Sputnik of October 1957 blazed its trail in the skies above us and the West woke up with a start at the news of such an unprecedented Russian achievement, still the sudden respect of the West for Soviet science and technology lasted only a few years, until America's astronauts caught up with Russia's cosmonauts, until this country overtook the Soviet Union and finally, in 1969, won the moon race when American men landed on that celestial body.

The historical fact is that even in her literature and music, so well known outside Russia nowadays, that country had a slow start. England gave Shakespeare to the world back in the sixteenth century, Germany introduced Beethoven in the eighteenth century, but it was only in the nineteenth century that Russia brought forth her great writers and composers. And Russia's scientists, although remarkable, seemed few and far between even as the twentieth century was dawning.

Science and technology in Russia made their first steps in the eighteenth century, and for a long time they appeared to be so very timid and not at all in full stride.

There was no science and little technology in old Russia until Czar Peter the Great, in the 1700s, hacked open that famous window into Europe. For centuries before his time, neither native curiosity nor foreign talent was given enough stretch and scope to inquire and speculate on matters outside theology; to research (if we may use a modern term about those ancient times) and to invent; to dabble even in such pseudosciences of the Middle Ages as alchemy and astrology, less so in their sounder realms of, say, Aristotelian philosophy or Arab mathematics.

Two phenomena of Russian history were responsible for this absence. The first was the fact that when Christianity came to Kiev in the tenth century, its point of origin was Byzantium; and its nature was utterly and narrowly dogmatic. The kind of Christianity the Byzantine Greeks brought to the Eastern Slavs consisted mostly of ritual and pageantry, which added to—but did not raise meaningfully—the primitive paganism of the aborigines. The dogma was frozen once and for all; and no fresh Western winds of the Renaissance were allowed to disturb it into any questioning and variance. How differently Russian culture might have evolved had Christianity been brought there from the West, not Byzantium! As it was fated to be, however, anything written or printed in Latin was for centuries (until Peter) regarded with suspicion.

The second historical reason was the Mongol invasion of, and yoke over, Russia from 1240 to 1480. The Mongols laid the country waste, stifled its growth, and deepened its isolation from Western Europe, while at the same time they failed to bring to the Russians whatever Chinese or other Oriental boons of civilization they could have carried with them but did not.

Moreover, if any class or feature of ancient Russia was spared by these Tatars, it was the Russian Orthodox Church; and its bishops, priests, and monks, while saving through their privileges whatever of national consciousness and achievements could be saved, did, on the whole, continue their active distaste for, and opposition to, Western thought and skills. Even after the Mongols grew weak and were finally defeated and pushed back east and after Russia at last was a sovereign state once more, the czars of Muscovy would not deviate from the old Byzantine habit of suspecting anything Western.

So theocratic and autocratic had the rule become that the rest of the nation, all the classes below the czars and the grand dukes, all the boyars, the bishops, and the priests, down to the vast masses of peasants, were anti-Western as well as non-Western. When in the early 1700s Czar Peter turned his kingdom Westward, the whole nation had to be dragged in that new direction (as has been so well said) by the scruff of its neck, kicking and screaming.

Not that Peter was breaking any vacuums. Already in ancient Muscovy some Italian architects had been brought in—to build if not to teach. In the seventeenth century Peter's father, Czar Alexis, invited German apothecaries; Dutch boatbuilders; and Scotch, Swedish, and other West European military mercenaries. But these were craftsmen, not scientists. And it has been said of Peter himself, and rightly, that with his heroic sweep of reforms, he was importing into Russia not so much Western civilization, as Western technology. That which was practical and immediately usable, rather than abstractly pathfinding, was of prime interest even to this mental wizard among Russia's czars.

Significantly, the Academy of Sciences, with its emphasis on pure research as well as pragmatic enlightenment, was founded by Peter as late as 1724, one year before he died. After its establishment, German and other foreign scientists manned it for decades; and the Russian language was rarely used in its learned halls. The first remarkable Russian scientist, Mikhail Lomonosov, although owing his emergence to Peter's spirit of innovation, developed after the czar's demise—and was, essentially, a lone figure all his life.

II

Today the Western man in the street knows little or nothing of science and technology in prerevolutionary Russia. Beginning with the Sputnik headlines of 1957, the average Westerner has acquired his current notion that before 1917 and the coming of the Soviet regime, Russia was a twilight land of hardly any schooling and no scientific achievements.

Actually, even Soviet propagandists have never seriously claimed that Russia's science owes everything to the Revolution of November 1917. In fact, anxious to ascribe practically every discovery and invention to their nation's early and inherent genius, they have often gone to the ludicrous extreme of asserting that old czarist scientists were ahead of their Western colleagues in this breakthrough or that.

In their calmer moments, the Soviets merely point to such great names as Mikhail Lomonosov, the eighteenth-century genius of physics and chemistry as well as linguistics; to Nikolai Lobachevsky of geometry and Dmitry Mendeleyev of chemistry in the nineteenth century; to Ilya Mechnikov of bacteriology, Konstantin Tsiolkovsky of rocketry, and Ivan Pavlov of physiology, who straddled both the nineteenth and early twentieth centuries.

But Soviet propagandists do allege that the oldtime czarists and their capitalists never truly encouraged that era's scientists and also that dastardly foreign entrepreneurs were too often allowed to steal or unduly exploit Russian insights and inventions. Yet, see how tenderly we Soviets foster our science and scientists!

A more sensible Soviet dictum is that whereas the scientists and other intellectuals of czarist times were fine, they were rare rays of light on the bleak Russian landscape. Giants of thought and achievement, they towered over the vast extent of the people's ignorance and sluggishness. But see the high level of popular education now, bringing forth and upwards the best in this talented Russian people!

The enigma of the Russians continues: What is the true state and future of Soviet science and technology? Are the Russians really so brilliant that they can overtake us and leave us behind even in the fields where they and we are on par now or where they still lag? Is there something in the soil of their country, in the soul of their nation, that makes for a unique and inevitable genius?

Or is there no inherent talent in that land and its people? Are the Russians merely and laughably frauds, a lot of Red copycats, clumsy with machines but adept at camouflage and propaganda, from whom no real competition will ever come to plague us—once we rectify our own few errors and lapses and generally put our ailing society in order?

On this subject, there have been among us several schools of appraisal and attitude, running the gamut from very little admiration for, or fear of, Russian ability to entirely too much respect for, or fright of, it.

At the gory dawn of the Soviet dictatorship, on his return from a trip to Russia and a talk with Vladimir Lenin in 1920, H. G. Wells wrote skeptically of Lenin's scheme to socialize Russia through electrification, to industrialize that nation via a tremendous network of powerhouses. To Wells, amid the nightmare he saw in Russia, Lenin's scheme was an eerie, unrealistic dream. Courageous, he said, yes, but totally implausible in this "vast flat land of forests and illiterate peasants, with no water power, with no technical skill available, and with trade and industry at the last gasp." Wells said as much to Lenin: "I cannot see anything of the sort happening in this dark crystal of Russia."

Lenin squinted stubbornly, as was his wont. "Come back and see what we have done in Russia in ten years' time," he replied to Wells.

By 1930—and 1940 and 1950—there were Stalinist terror and misery and seeming chaos as the most logical sequence to Lenin's disorder of mind and matter. But in seven more years, by 1957, it suddenly appeared as if Lenin had been right about the inherent quality of Russian technical genius, after all. When the first Sputnik beep-beep sounded around the world, a physicist at the Massachusetts Institute of Technology mused aloud, "When I feel really gloomy, I think that five years from now the Russians will be ahead of us in every area. But when I feel optimistic, I think it may take them ten."

From the bottom of the bottom, those fantastic Russians were all at once ascending to the very top of the human heap. From our disbelief or sneer to alarm and even panic—such has been the short, awful road we traveled in our approach to Russia's scientific and technical capacity.

For too long a time we had thought that the Soviet terrorism would hinder those scientists—their freedom, their initiative—too much for them to come up in their research with anything of worth. It did not dawn upon us until lately that the Soviet diversion of money and manpower from consumer goods to a scientific crash program could, on occasion, outweigh the terroristic disadvantage of totalitarianism.

III

When, not so long ago, the West denied the Russians any scientific-technical knack at all, the Soviets unwittingly helped this notion. For so many years they had, especially in Josef Stalin's era, made their ridiculous claims to having invented everything from the wheel to radar and from the slingshot to the atom-splitter that the West came to dismiss any Russian ingenuity as bluff.

". . . the Soviet diversion of money and manpower
from consumer goods to a scientific program" is
typified by these Muscovites queuing up for street
purchases in 1969. *Sovfoto*

The alleged July 20, 1882 flight of Alexander
Mozhaisky's airplane on the outskirts of St.
Petersburg. The portrait is of Mozhaisky. *Sovfoto*

We used to jest about it with a marvelous feeling of superiority to
those arrogant yokels, who, we thought, did not know enough even
to use handkerchiefs instead of the sleeves of their red blouses. You
will recall the typical joke about Andrei Gromyko, the Soviet minister of foreign affairs: He walks into a New York exhibition hall, sees
our latest industrial gadgets and gimmicks, rubs his hands in glee,
and exclaims, "Look at all the things we are going to invent!"

The Soviet authorities seemed to prove our point beyond their
evil cavil when, apparently unable to evolve the atomic bomb on
their own fast enough, they saved time by "borrowing" certain of
the bomb's secrets from us.

True, it took their scientists disquietingly fewer years than we
allowed them to achieve the first atomic explosion even with the aid
of their espionage and our turncoats' treason that delivered our
secrets to them. Our first atomic explosion was brought off on July
16, 1945. Theirs occurred on September 22, 1949. The gap was
closed in little more than four years, an uncomfortably short (for us)
time.

Still they dulled our anxiety with those extravagant Soviet claims of the 1940s. Although they did not say they were the first to invent the atomic bomb, they did declare that they were the originators of atomic fission. This made us laugh, and we felt better and safe—until August 12, 1953, when they exploded their first hydrogen bomb only nine and one-half months after the first American H-Bomb was detonated (November 1, 1952) and by methods not borrowed from us but all their own.

Generally, however, their scientific pretense has always seemed far greater than their performance. The last decade of Stalin's reign was particularly marked by xenophobia and its concomitant outburst of chauvinistic claims to almost every discovery and invention in man's history. From the middle 1940s till Stalin's death in March 1953, they declared their priority in practically all the world's firsts. They had, they said, a veritable corner on human genius. If ever there was a case for the Russians' natural inventiveness, the Soviets spoiled it by claiming genius that simply could not exist—certainly not in such overwhelming, all-embracing doses.

Their list was long, and it began early. There was, the Soviets proclaimed, that eighteenth-century colossus Lomonosov, who discovered the conservation of matter and energy, the composition of the atmosphere of Venus, the theory of evolution, and the initial principles of the helicopter.

A wizard named Yefim Artamonov allegedly invented the bicycle in 1800. Next year (the Russians now say) he pedaled his wondrous two-wheeler a thousand miles from his native Urals to Moscow to demonstrate it at the coronation of Czar Alexander I, some four decades ahead of any pedal-pushing done by Kirkpatrick McMillan of Scotland, who in the West is usually given the world's first bicycle laurels.

This was followed in 1819–1821 by the discovery of Antarctica, not by Captain James Cook or any insolent Yankee whaler, but, says Moscow, by the Russian expedition under Faddei Bellingshausen and Mikhail Lazarev.

Then, in the 1870s, Thomas Alva Edison stole the electric lamp from two Russian scientists, Alexander Lodyghin and Pavel Yablochkov. Either willfully or thoughtlessly, czarist officials had revealed the secret to the American. "In 1877 in America, Lieutenant Khotinsky showed an electric lamp to Edison as a Russian miracle," *Izvestia* complained in March 1948, adding spitefully: "And yet, it took Edison seven more years to produce a lamp."

Not the Wright brothers in 1903, but Alexander Mozhaisky in 1882, invented the plane and flew it. Marconi pilfered the radio from Alexander Popov, who, on May 7, 1895, staged before his fellow physicists the first demonstration of wireless telegraphy. May 7 is now Radio Day in the Soviet Union. Books, films, monuments glorify Popov. As for television, according to the Soviets, in 1911 Professor Boris L. Rosing of Russia proved to be ahead of the scientists of America, England, and Germany by ten to fifteen years.

At the height of the Stalinist mania of claims, the list of technological achievements where Russia allegedly showed the West the way included also: the adding machine, the agricultural combine, anesthesia, armored cruisers, balloons, baseball, the caterpillar tractor, chemical dyeing, crop rotation, diesel-engine improvements, electroplating, the flashlight, gunpowder, hybrid corn, icebreakers, jet propulsion, the loop-the-loop in aviation, minefields installed under water, oil derricks and oil-cracking processes, the parachute, penicillin, printing machinery, radar, railways, relativity, rockets of the multistage variety, roller bearings, rolled armor plate, the steam engine, steel girders, the submarine (armored), tanks, the telegraph, textile-making machines, torpedoes, trawlers, virus discoveries, vitamins, and welding.

In sum, the West hardly ever discovered or invented anything, but always filched from the clever, hardworking Russians. At their feeble best, Western inventors were Johnnies-come-lately, shamefully ignorant of the Russian priority.

IV

The overwhelming, wholesale claim came rather late in the Soviet season, and quite suddenly. Until it came, the Soviet claim of progress, of a monopoly on wisdom and virtue, had been confined to sociopolitical matters. Throughout the 1920s and 1930s, and, in fact, well into the 1940s, Russian Communists and their foreign friends or admirers had sadly recognized that in the precise sciences and technology the West was well ahead of the Soviet republic, which admittedly needed time to catch up.

At no point would the Soviets accept any blame for the conceded lag or lack. Instead, the Soviet government always denounced its czarist predecessor for keeping the nation so underindustrialized, so backward in machinery. With a curious mixture of vigor and hysteria, the Kremlin promised to nullify the gap. "To overtake and outstrip America," was the favorite Soviet motto.

And then, about 1947, came the sudden switch which proclaimed, in effect: "We Russians are not so backward after all and, what is more, never were. Not only will we lead the world's science and technology—we have always been in its vanguard."

The purposes of this drastic change in the Soviet line were several: The change served to reassure or convince the Russians and their satellites that Russia was the best country on earth. This barrage of claims implied that the Russian people had much more intelligence, initiative, and ingenuity than the people of any other nation in the world.

The new line was also to spread and strengthen antagonism toward the West, particularly toward America. Besides, Stalin hoped that this burst of freshly discovered scientific glory would inspire Soviet scientists and engineers to new epoch-making achievements. On the levels below the technological elite, the man in the factory and on the farm would be spurred to further and harder effort at his machine by his awakened pride in all this complex technology as rightfully of Russian origin.

But few intelligent Russians nodded any solemn assent to this campaign, less so lent any fervent belief and aid. And while foreign ridicule of the "Russians-were-there-first" campaign did not appear to bother the Kremlin, it was different when Soviet subjects, openly or not, made sport of the claims. Soviet propagandists were occasionally rebuked for overdoing the claims to the point of absurdity evident at home even more than abroad. On May 31, 1949, *Izvestia* castigated Vsevolod Ivanov for his latest play on Lomonosov, in which the eighteenth-century scientist is built up by so many overenthusiastic historical blunders that "our cause of struggling for the priority of Russian science is not at all served."

If Vsevolod Ivanov's stumbles were merely the result of his excess of zeal, other public entertainers were far more deliberate. Late in

June 1949, Leonid Utesov, a leading Moscow entertainer with a term of exile for past misdeeds behind him, risked one more punishment when he mounted the stage with an umbrella and a straight man. "Congratulate me, I have just invented the umbrella," he cracked. "But the umbrella was invented by the Chinese centuries ago!" protested Comrade Stooge. "Yes," Utesov rejoined, "but I am the first to invent the umbrella the second time!"

Then there was the Soviet story of an American visitor who was perplexed by hearing everywhere he went in the Soviet Union about the two great Russian inventors, Orlov and Stavrov. They were, it seemed, the root-source of all the inventions that separated the world from the Dark Ages. Curious, the American started making inquiries about Orlov, for it was said that Orlov invented the telephone, the telegraph, the printing press, the electric light, the steam engine, the internal combustion engine, as well as radio, television, the automobile, and inside plumbing. Yes, everybody agreed, Orlov invented all these things, but he was only the second greatest Russian inventor. But who was the first greatest Russian inventor, pray? "Why, that was Stavrov." Oh, so. And what did he invent? "Ah, he invented Orlov."

V

Somewhere between this overestimation and this ridicule lies the actual truth. There is a case for the Russians' inherent ingenuity, but for a time the Soviets obscured it by pretending an all-embracing greatness that just was not possible in any nation at any point in history. Thus they have cast a shadow on, and caused our doubts about, the genuine achievements that do exist on the credit side of their scientific and engineering ledgers.

But is this technical ability something brand-new? Or did it slumber, hidden, at the long-ago dawn of the nation's industrialization and mechanization? Some foreign observers said years back that, yes, it was right there; that on occasion you could even then chance upon it, accidentally.

Back in the early 1900s, this native technical skill of the Russians was noticed by a clear-eyed American visitor—Simon Lake, the man from New Jersey who perfected the early submarine.

On bringing his blueprints to Russia, he voiced his awe for the quick, smart ways of the Russians detailed by the czar to help the American to build those newfangled undersea boats for the Russian navy. While working in a St. Petersburg shipyard, he needed a bronze sleeve to fit over a reversible propeller. It was one of Lake's patents. He was the first to use it on a large boat. To quote from Lake's reminiscences:

> I knew I could not get the sleeve I needed from the United States in time to do me any good, I might never be able to get it from England, and yet the fact remained that I had to have it right away. The manager of a Russian foundry said, "Let me make it for you, Gospodin Simon."
> I thought he was talking through his hat, but I was willing to listen.
> "I'll have it for you at four o'clock tomorrow morning."
> I knew that was nonsense, even if he did not. The best American maker might not be able to make that sleeve in less than two or three weeks. But he put his experts to work overnight and the sleeve was ready for me in the morning, a perfect piece.

Lake also found that the Russians cast steel in better ways than Americans could, and he saw "cast steel go under a planer and a shaving turned off one-eighth of an inch thick, one-quarter of an inch wide, and as long as you wanted it."

Simon Lake concluded: "I am somewhat puzzled by the reports of the apparent ineptitude of the Russians in dealing with mechanical matters. I found them excellent mechanics, for the most part, and in some things they were ahead of us."

What foreign observers, in times of both czars and commissars, often mistook for the lack of an inherent technical ability was really the presence of too many mistakes in technical organization. Yet habits should not be judged as native ability, and vice versa. True, in many fields of endeavor, Russia has horrible habits of work, bad distribution of tasks, overstaffing, nepotism. But all this is gross inefficiency rather than insufficiency of talent. There is a difference.

A striking comparison of Russian ways of work with American was given in the 1890s by a Russian nobleman-intellectual, Pyotr Dementyev, who, having settled in this country and changed his name to Peter Demens, is remembered at least in Florida as the founder of the city that he christened St. Petersburg after the capital of his native land. He quoted a Russian artisan, bedridden in a California hospital: "In Russia we are used to taking it easy as we work. We drag out our jobs. But here they make everyone as much as boil at work. No chance to loiter on the job at all." Demens agreed, expanding the point:

> Russian working ways cannot even be compared to American ones. An American works intensively, energetically, with more strength and effort. But then he is better fed than a worker in Russia. He works some eight or ten hours a day, not thirteen or eighteen as I myself used to see people work in my old homeland. The American worker is more intelligent and progressive than the Russian muzhik. He is not at all conservative in his methods of work as the Russian is. He works not with his muscle alone but with his brain, too, economizing in his exertion wherever possible. He does not try to move a wall by battering it with his . forehead. Nor does he throw his weight around needlessly.

That is why, observed the Russian in America, the American way of life and work was "out of the question for an average Russian."

In the early 1900s, the same Simon Lake who praised the technical skill found in so many Russians spoke in astonishment about the indolent, irregular habits of their work. At the New Admiralty Works in St. Petersburg, he began to suspect that not all the fifteen hundred men he was employing to build his submarines for the czar were doing an honest day's toil. He found that many workmen did check in for work, but only about one half of the number could be found on the jobs. He tried an experiment: "One day I had the whistle sounded for quitting work, and I watched the yards from a little balcony at the machine shop. Men crawled out from abandoned buildings and old lumber-piles like ants and hurried to check in with the timekeeper."

Even as machines were brought into Russia, their worth was impaired by the barbaric lack of care, by the failure to have spare parts at the right time and place, and by doing too many auxiliary tasks around the machine, not with an additional mechanism but with wasteful manual labor. In Soviet farming, in particular, many a machine is reduced in its usefulness time and again when one of its functions is still done by hand. On his trip to Russia in 1955, United States Supreme Court Justice William O. Douglas saw that at a fanning mill, where grain was cleaned, many peasant women carried the grain in baskets from piles on the ground to the machine's hopper. Wrote Mr. Douglas, rightly: "The labor saving of the machine is lost by the absence of mechanical means to lift the grain from the ground to the hopper."

We have heard, we have read, that tremendous combines cut and thresh the grain on those great Russian plains. But we also know that the straw in the wake of those mechanized operations is still being stacked by hand. Or take Soviet dairies. On most Soviet dairy farms, the milking is done by machines, but the feeding of these cows is done by hand—slowly, clumsily, and by too many hands per cow.

Often in Russia's steppes today, a horse-drawn wagon follows a machine to do what another machine, not a wagon, should really do. And that horse-drawn wagon is full of peasants, mostly women, who are there to do all the raking and lifting and hauling—far too many "workers" for the job. And far too many bosses, brigadiers, inspectors, directors, and bookkeepers give them orders and keep track of what is done and not done—an old Russian custom of too many drones for too few bees.

What is true of Russian agriculture is also true, albeit to a somewhat lesser degree, of Russian cities and industry. In late 1969, Dr. Irving S. Bengelsdorf, the Russian-speaking science writer for the Los Angeles *Times*, visiting Moscow as a guest of the Academy of Sciences, watched a snow-removal crew laboring in the streets around the Kremlin walls: "There was a modern, automatic snow plow, with crab-like claws in front gathering in the snow as the plow advanced. But, in front of the moving claws walked two women with brooms pushing the snow into the plow."

An American metallurgist marveled at the tremendous growth of Soviet metallurgy, yet in no Soviet factory or laboratory did he notice anyone wearing safety goggles. He did see "a lot of Russians in bandages." In the Moscow *Krokodil* there is an admission that "new and powerful hoisting mechanisms at various plants are used not for the purposes for which they are designed." A cartoon shows a thirty-ton, weight-lifting crane, operated by a woman worker, in the act of hoisting some ridiculously tiny hardware. *Izvestia* quotes workers of a casting department in a Moscow machine shop: "To make one good machine part we have to produce from ten to fifteen of them, until finally, quite by accident, we do get one good one."

VI

Zemlia nasha obil'na, poriadka tol'ko net. This old, famous Russian line can be rendered: "We have much good stuff in our nation; the only thing lacking is order." Autocracy without order? Totalitarianism with no efficiency? Chaos despite the iron rule of czars and steel rule of commissars? Incredible, but true. Only by a superhuman effort of a crash-through program can Russia achieve heights such as she has recently won in the field of rockets and missiles.

But because for centuries there has been poor organization of the wonderfully good resources of nature's wealth and of human brain and muscle, Russia arrives late and only after a wasteful effort; and her arrival is greeted as an unbelievable miracle.

Because the masses of her people and the ways of her life have for generations been so backward, we in the West do not always recognize the inherent talent of that nation. Nor do we pay timely heed to the clear-cut historic record of the best of the scientists she has contributed to the modern world, a record that should have prepared us for the news of the sputniks but, alas, did not.

Obviously, even in the amazing campaign of the middle and late 1940s, not all of the Kremlin claims were lies. A few of the assertions were based on facts, even though the superstructure of the claim was sham. Lomonosov *was* a great scientist, whose worth should have been recognized a long time ago. We should have remembered the brilliance of the nineteenth-century names and deeds of Nikolai Lobachevsky in geometry and Dmitry Mendeleyev in chemistry. The first plant virus was indeed discovered by Dmitry Ivanovsky, and soil research owes its beginnings to Dmitry Prianishnikov. The much-traveled Lord Frederic Hamilton saw his first oil-burning steamer not on the Thames, the Mississippi, or the Rhine, but on the Volga; and he wrote about it with wonder.

In rocket work Konstantin Tsiolkovsky anticipated, at least in some respects, Germany's Hermann Oberth and our own Robert H. Goddard. Popov was praised by Marconi himself. And Lodyghin was welcomed to Pittsburgh by Westinghouse in the 1890s as the result of his foreign patents for the incandescent lamp. Before dying in Brooklyn in 1923 at seventy-five, Lodyghin had the satisfaction of seeing recognition of his pioneer use of wolfram, molybdenum, and osmium filaments in the electric lamp.

It was Igor Sikorsky who brought his better helicopter from Russia and built that giant aircraft factory in Connecticut. And such American concerns as Westinghouse and the RCA company appreciated Vladimir K. Zworykin's contributions to practical electronics.

But these two—and many other Russian scientists and engineers in Western lands—were émigrés who fled the intolerable totalitarianism of the Reds. We knew, of course, that many other Russian scientists could not or would not flee Russia. We also realized that Russia's schools and laboratories were training new generations of engineers and scientists.

Soviet statistics show that if in 1897 all the Russian intellectuals numbered only 700,000, in 1926 there were three times as many; and in 1966 there were 26 million. Of the 233,000,000 Soviet inhabitants in 1966, 80,300,000 possessed high or middle education of all kinds, scientific and nonscientific. The Soviet Union's industrial production rose from less than 30 percent of the United States' production in 1950 to 65 percent of it in 1966. Productivity of labor in 1967 was 16 times that of 1913 in general, and 23 times higher per hour. It was announced in 1969 that the highest Moscow authorities in charge of inventions received 100,000 applications for patents annually. The grand goal, that of catching up with and overtaking America, was quite within the Soviet sight, or such was the confident aim.

Strong and growing, indeed, is the scientific establishment of the Soviet Union, the base of this bright hope. The latest official Moscow figures available, for the end of 1970, show a total of 4,985 higher scientific and educational organizations (including 2,458 research institutes), manned by 927,700 "scientific workers," that is, academicians (members of the Soviet Academy of Sciences, highest-ranking savants), professors, *dotsenty* (lecturers), research associates and assistants, and other staff members. This overall figure represents "one quarter of all the scientific workers of the world."

The Soviets agree with Western statistics that the general number of highly skilled scientific workers in the USSR is presently about the same as that of the USA. They admit that this shows a Soviet lag if only because the Soviet Union's population is larger than that of the United States. But the Soviets insist that their regime has done well: in their reports the Soviet figures are usually contrasted with the much smaller numbers of Russian scientists and their assistants known to exist on the eve of the Revolution of 1917.

We can, of course, raise the objection that in the past half century, many another country's science and technology have also grown without the dubious benefit of a socialist regime and that Russia, too, would have progressed in this respect even if there had been no Vladimir Lenin and his take-over of the nation.

VII

Impressive though such statistics may be, we may also legitimately ask: What content of free scientific inquiry is there beneath such numbers? How sincerely are the Soviet rulers devoted to the higher ideals of science?

About one-half of the Soviet era, 1917–1973, was Stalin's period, marked by the suppression, oppression, and depression of Russia's sciences and scientists. Stalin's time was particularly hard on Mendelian genetics, cybernetics, the Einstein theory of relativity, quantum physics, mathematical logic, finitary cosmological theories, sociometry, and psychoanalytic studies.

Cruelest hit were the Mendelians. They were persecuted and arrested, and many killed by Stalin's order on the psychotic say-so of Trofim Lysenko, the dictator's pet and pseudoscholar who insisted that acquired characteristics could be handed down from generation to generation. Though perhaps a talented botanist with a green thumb and a considerable knowledge of Russian soil, climate, and seed, Lysenko—in his huge appetite for celebrity, comforts, and petty power—did not hesitate to make preposterous claims, violating the most obvious precepts of genetics, just so that Stalin would applaud and reward him. This was how scores of reputable Russian scientists lost their jobs—and many, their liberty and their very lives—when they dared to oppose Lysenko, even if mildly.

And so Nikolai Vavilov, the greatest plant geneticist of his time, winner of the Lenin Prize in 1926, arrested in 1940, was to die in a prison in 1943. Nor was Nikolai Vavilov the first Russian geneticist to perish. In 1935, I. J. Agol and L. P. Ferry were the first Mendelians to be shot by the Soviet secret police. In 1937, N. P. Avdulov, a cytologist, was put to death after five years in a concentration camp. The same year the Soviet police executed S. G. Levit, former head of the celebrated Moscow Institute for Medical Genetic Research. Nor is this numbing list complete: Whole staffs of anti-Lysenko geneticists died similarly, in prisons and labor camps, of quick bullets or slow mistreatment.

In citing one more instance of brutality and harm done in the Stalin era to Russian science and engineering, let us recall that Andrei N. Tupolev, one of that nation's most gifted aircraft designers, the originator of the world-renowned TU series of planes, among them some of the world's largest and fastest passenger airliners, was also once a prisoner and a slave. He spent five years—1938 to 1943—in a Soviet jail, and it was there that he and his staff were compelled to design one of his planes.

It was only in 1968, with the publication of Alexander Solzhenitsyn's *The First Circle*, that the world learned the full horror of *sharashki*, the special prisons for Soviet professors and engineers, complete with laboratories behind the bars, in which Stalin for years kept some of the nation's best scientific and technical talent. Stalin's heirs in the Kremlin frown upon such revelations: as of now, although circulating throughout the world in numberless copies in many languages, this book by Solzhenitsyn is still banned in the Soviet Union.

By this time, certain of the political relaxations introduced by Nikita Khrushchev in the eleven years of his rule (1953–1964) have been withdrawn, and Russian scientists are among the sufferers. In late May 1970, just a month after celebrating the centenary of Lenin's birth, the Soviet leaders Leonid Brezhnev and Alexei Kosygin ordered the arrest of Zhores A. Medvedev, a prominent biologist. This was the first detention of an outstanding Soviet scientist since Stalin's times, but by no means the first repression directed by the post-Stalin and post-Khrushchev rulers against the nation's scholarly community.

Beginning with the latter 1960s, by slow but certain degrees, contacts between Soviet scholars and their foreign colleagues have been lessened and, in many cases, altogether forbidden. Delegations of Soviet scientists to international congresses are suddenly, at the very last moment, ordered to stay home, much to their embarrassment and chagrin and to their foreign friends' and session chairmen's dismay.

On the lower levels, younger and less known scientists and engineers are questioned by the secret police as to their political views and activities, their homes and laboratories are searched, their books and papers are confiscated, and they themselves are dismissed from their jobs and barred from anything but menial employment. Some are arrested and tried, usually in secret, and sentenced to concentration camps, prisons, and, increasingly, insane asylums—this last apparently on some such premise as "You don't like the Soviet regime? You must be crazy."

In sum, the process of re-Stalinization seems to be in full swing and sway at present. A far cry this is indeed from the halcyon days of 1960, when Khrushchev's de-Stalinization seemed to be irrevocable, nay, a promise of yet further thaw to come. The Soviet Union may yet relive the blood and tears shed by the nation and its scholars in 1930, 1940, and 1950—those worst years of Stalin's era. We can almost hear the tragic whisper, "This is where we came in."

PART I
Great Names in Russian Science

1. MIKHAIL LOMONOSOV
One-Man University

WITH much solemnity and pride, the Soviet Union celebrated in 1961 the 250th anniversary of Mikhail Lomonosov's birth. Yet the Western world barely noticed the excitement. Volume 25 of the *Great Soviet Encyclopedia* devotes more than fourteen pages to this famous Russian scientist. Western encyclopedias give him a scant paragraph or two.

The Soviets have named their foremost university, the University of Moscow, in Lomonosov's honor. Late in 1959, after photographing the far side of the moon with Lunik III, they gave his name to one of its craters. Russian textbooks speak of the Lomonosov law instead of the Lavoisier law. A mineral claimed as a Soviet discovery is called lomonosovite.

Near Leningrad, the Baltic seashore town of Oranienbaum, remarkable for the beauty of its eighteenth-century palaces and parks, has been renamed Lomonosov. Biographies and novels have been written about him in Russia; plays have been staged, and films produced, on his life and work. Still, the West knows little about Lomonosov.

Physicist, chemist, astronomer, meteorologist, geologist, metallurgist, inventor, historian, artist, poet, playwright, reformer of the Russian language, founder of the University of Moscow (Russia's first), one of the earliest pillars of the Academy of Sciences, Mikhail Lomonosov has been hailed increasingly by the Russians for more than two centuries as the beginner of all their modern learning, as their patron saint of all sciences and nearly all arts. The Russians today are hurt and puzzled at Western neglect of him.

They claim much for him. They insist that this eighteenth-century genius was among the first to discuss atoms intelligently and also the first to discover the law of the conservation of matter and energy, the initial principles of the helicopter, and the presence of an atmosphere around the planet Venus.

Mikhail (Michael) was born on November 19, 1711, on an island near Arkhangelsk on the White Sea, the son of a prosperous peasant-fisherman-shipper. The time and the place were significant.

Czar Peter I, later called "the Great," was hardly ever on his throne. He was off fighting the Swedes and the Turks for exits to western and southern seas and forcing Westernization upon his bewildered, reluctant people. Western learning was on a pedestal, and Western technology was prodigiously hired or bought by Peter.

The northern White Sea was then one of the few war-spared avenues to the West. Foreign merchants and goods came to Russia via Arkhangelsk. It was a freer, prouder part of Russia than many another. Here the Mongol yoke of past centuries had been unknown, and serfdom was not practiced.

Lomonosov's family were *pomory*, which means "seacoast dwellers"—peasants but not serfs. Not all of them were well-to-do, yet they were never as impoverished as was the general run of the Russian peasantry. They were independent and intensely curious about the world beyond the horizon of the White Sea.

II

Vasily, Mikhail's father, sent his firstborn to a literate neighbor to learn reading and writing when the boy was six. At ten, Mikhail began an apprenticeship on his father's ship, the *Seagull*. Between the voyages, the lad read and sang holy texts at church services. Later, Mikhail would retell the psalms and saints' lives to old men

Moscow State University, founded in 1755 by Mikhail Lomonosov, has long been the intellectual and scientific center of Russia. *Novosti from Sovfoto*

sitting in a refectory. His verve and his memory amazed the audience.

At fourteen, Mikhail borrowed a Slavonic grammar and Leonty F. Magnitsky's *Arithmetic*. Again and again, he read both volumes. The newly famous Magnitsky volume was not only on arithmetic. It also contained introductory material on geometry, physics, astronomy, geography, navigation, architecture, and the art and science of building fortifications. Lomonosov later called this encyclopedic book "the gate to my learning."

Mikhail's mother had died in his infancy. His father had remarried twice, and now the second stepmother plagued the youth's existence. A bitter, jealous woman, she disliked his bookishness; so in December 1730, at nineteen, Mikhail left his island village.

First with one caravan of fish-laden sledges, then with another, he rode and walked the hundreds of frozen miles to Moscow. In January 1731, with the aid of friends, he entered the eight-year course of Moscow's Slavo-Greco-Latin Academy.

Peasants' sons were barred from such schools, and Mikhail boldly misrepresented himself as the offspring of a northern nobleman. The deception was in time discovered—and forgiven. His father refused to send him any help, although Vasily's shipping and fishing prospered and there were still no other children in the Lomonosov family. The school gave Mikhail a stipend of three kopecks a day. On this Spartan allowance Mikhail half-starved for years.

He studied with a will and with brilliance, finishing the first two years of the course in one year. His Latin was soon so good that he wrote letters, scientific papers, and even brief poems in it; and his Greek was not far behind.

Early in 1736, a call came from the government to the Moscow Academy to send twenty of its best students from the advanced classes to the Academic *ghimnaziya* (secondary school) at St. Petersburg. Only twelve such students could be found, and Lomonosov was at the very top of the list of those chosen.

However, this particular stay in St. Petersburg was not long. In the fall of 1736, the government sent him and two other students to Germany. They were to go first to the University of Marburg, there to study chemistry, physics, and the German and French languages.

Then they were to move on to Freiberg for an intensive study of chemistry, mining, and metallurgy.

At Marburg, the trio's main teacher was Professor Christian Wolff, a mathematician and philosopher. He singled out Lomonosov as the most capable student of the three and helped him considerably. Lomonosov repaid him with admiration and later translated and published in Russia some of Wolff's theories and experiments in physics; but he disagreed with Wolff's naive metaphysics, although he was grateful to the German for introducing him to the works of Descartes, Newton, and Leibniz.

The Marburg sojourn was not all study, however. Lomonosov joined his two fellow Russians in heavy drinking and idle philandering. All three ran up high debts, which Wolff had to pay for them (he was later reimbursed by the czarist government).

Having heard of their dissolute ways in Marburg, their Freiberg professor, Johann Henckel, greeted them with a regime of financial and disciplinary supervision. Lomonosov might have stood for this, but the discovery of how backward Henckel was in his views on chemistry and how intolerant he was of any disagreement with them, disturbed him greatly. Lomonosov stopped coming to Henckel's lectures and finally, in May 1740, fled from Freiberg.

Penniless, he went to Leipzig and from there, with friends' help, to Kassel, seeking whatever funds he might beg from the Russian ambassador. Unable to find the envoy, he made his way to Marburg, where, on June 6, 1740, he secretly married a German girl, Elizabeth Zilch, whom he had known in his three years there. The marriage remained a secret from both the authorities and his friends for a number of years.

Then, alone and still penniless, he journeyed through Germany and Holland, searching for Russian envoys and funds, in order to return to St. Petersburg. At one point, tired and hungry, he wandered into a Prussian tavern, where a hussar officer, a recruiter, eyed the Russian's tall, powerful figure, invited him to dinner, and got him drunk. Lomonosov awoke to find himself a soldier of the Prussian king. He pretended to submit, but planned his escape carefully. Several nights later, he carried out his intention, fleeing from the fortress of Wessel, down the ramparts and across the moats, then over several miles of fields, just ahead of the cavalry that pursued him, until he was safe over the frontier into Westphalia. Thus, he once more arrived in Marburg.

It was in 1741 that money and permission—in fact, an order—to return to Russia reached him. In July of that year, he came back to St. Petersburg. Instead of punishment, he was given work.

Young men of learning were needed. A series of small jobs filled out the year: cataloguing minerals, translating newspapers, and writing poetry were part of his duties.

Early next year he received his first permanent appointment. From January 1742, he was an "adjunct in the physics class" at the Academy of Sciences. His annual salary was 360 rubles, but there was no money in the Academy's treasury. Instead, the academicians were permitted to buy books at nominal prices in the Academy's bookshop and then resell them at a profit.

Lomonosov's troubles were at this time aggravated by his drunken fights with his German colleagues at the Academy and with his German fellow tenants. Although he had some good friends among them, his enemies outnumbered them. The Russian patriot in him seethed with ire at the sight of the Academy's being staffed almost exclusively by foreigners.

The fights were not merely verbal. Lomonosov suffered severe wounds even as he inflicted injuries and abuse upon the Germans. He was arrested in May 1743, taken to the police station, then returned to his own quarters though still under detention, which lasted until January 1744. He was penalized a half-year's salary, made to apologize to his victims publicly, and warned against such conduct in the future. Indeed, never again did he permit himself such behavior. He had sent for his German wife, and she joined him later that year.

His frustration with his German superiors at the Academy was finally lessened when in 1745 he was allowed to defend his dissertation on metallurgy to gain the rank of professor. That year Lomonosov was named the Academy's professor of chemistry.

In 1746 the Imperial Senate decreed that he use the Russian language in his lectures. This was the day of rejoicing for him and all the other patriots of Russian science. Until then the academicians had lectured in either German or Latin.

Thus began his settled and truly productive life.

III

Russian biographers divide Lomonosov's scientific career into three parts. At first, he busied himself mainly with problems of physics. In 1748, overcoming bureaucratic and financial handicaps, he won for the Academy a chemical laboratory. There he worked on chemical projects until 1757, when the Academy's chemical professorship was given to another savant.

Lomonosov, at that time, transferred his work to his private laboratory. Then, until his death in 1765, he studied electricity, analyzed ore samples from all over Russia, experimented with formulas for making porcelain and stained glass, and tried his hand at mosaics and optics.

Through all the three periods, his interest in poetry, art, linguistics, and history never slackened. Clumsy as the rules on poetry and verse that he devised may appear now, they were a distinct innovation in, and improvement over, the Russian poetry of that era. His theories of versification left their mark on later poets.

His prose, however, had a simpler, yet more lasting, influence. The two tragedies he wrote at the czarina's command were successful, and the language of his scientific writing was fresh and agile. The great nineteenth-century Russian writer Alexander Pushkin emphatically acknowledged his generation's indebtedness to Lomonosov.

In 1743, Lomonosov wrote his celebrated treatise on Russian rhetoric. In 1755, he completed what is now considered the first scientific work on Russian grammar. Breaking away from the heavy Church Slavonic and its elaborate syntax, yet fusing some of its best elements with everyday speech, he laid the foundations of the modern Russian language. Similarly, he blazed the trail with his history of Russia, which the Academy published in 1760.

He also painted and drew. In his Academy speeches, he pronounced new ideas on the development of Russia's graphic arts. He helped several native artists to their first recognition.

Under him the art of Russian mosaics, forgotten since the twelfth century, was revived. He created mosaic pictures himself and trained others in the art. Of the forty mosaic portraits and panels done by Lomonosov and his aides, twenty-three are now reverently preserved in Soviet museums and galleries.

Московской здѣсь Парнассъ изобразилъ витію,
Что чистой слогъ стиховъ и прозы ввелъ въ Россію.
Что въ Римѣ Цицеронъ и что Виргилій былъ,
То онъ одинъ въ своемъ понятіи вмѣстилъ,
Открылъ натуры храмъ богатымъ словомъ Россовъ
Примѣръ ихъ остроты въ наукахъ Ломоносовъ.

Полное Собраніе

СОЧИНЕНІЙ

Михайла Васильевича

ЛОМОНОСОВА,

Съ пріобщеніемъ жизни сочинителя и съ прибавленіемъ

многихъ его нигдѣ еще не напечатанныхъ твореній.

Часть первая.

ВЪ САНКТПЕТЕРБУРГѢ,

иждивеніемъ Императорской Академіи Наукъ

1784 года.

Title page from 1784 edition of *The Complete Works of Mikhail V. Lomonosov,* with an engraved portrait of Lomonosov. *Sovfoto*

As one of the chief founders of the University of Moscow in 1755, he planned its entire policy. Two years later, Lomonosov was appointed a councillor of the Academy's chancellors; in 1758 he was entrusted with the "overseeing" of the Academy's Geographic Department, Historical Assembly, university, and ghimnaziya.

While continuing his work in physics, chemistry, astronomy, navigation, linguistics, mosaicking, and a dozen other sciences and arts, he still kept on planning, lecturing, and writing until the day of his death. This came in his fifty-fourth year on April 15, 1765. He was buried in St. Petersburg in the cemetery of the Monastery of Alexander Nevsky. The handsome though conventional tombstone is well kept. Throngs also stop to admire his monument erected by the Soviets in front of the skyscrapers of the University of Moscow in its new location in the Lenin Hills. In Leningrad crowds also visit the recently reconstructed Lomonosov Museum. This is in the old building of the Academy of Sciences, left vacant when the Soviets moved the venerable institution to Moscow.

The West had known about Lomonosov for a long time before it would afford him the least recognition as the great scientist that he was. The trouble, his Russian biographers explain, was that Lomonosov refused to publish his most remarkable discoveries and theories.

For this Lomonosov had two reasons. One was that such offerings were so revolutionary that both Russian and Western scientists of his era would have laughed and raged at him unless he presented more proof than he could have shown at the time. The other reason was Lomonosov's reluctance to sadden Professor Wolff's declining years. For Lomonosov's theories, if published, would surely have demolished the lifework of his beloved Marburg mentor.

During his lifetime Lomonosov never made public his atomic theories. In brief, these amounted to his belief that all matter consisted of minute particles, both compound and simple. He gave the name "corpuscle" to compound particles and the name "element" to their ingredients—to simple particles.

Lomonosov did publish in 1744, 1750, and 1760 papers on his theories and experiments demonstrating the natural law of the preservation of matter and motion. Russian scientists now point out that it was only in 1789 that Antoine Lavoisier of France published his findings on the preservation of the mass during chemical conversion.

The Russians argue that Lavoisier never credited himself with the discovery of the law of the preservation of matter. They maintain that although he failed to mention Lomonosov's earlier experiments, there is evidence that Lavoisier had read Lomonosov's *Meditations on the Origin of Heat and Cold* (first published in 1750) before he himself experimented with this problem.

Similarly, it was only in 1842 that the German physicist Julius Robert von Mayer published his mechanical theory of heat that is considered one of the first Western statements of the principle of the conservation of energy.

Professor Victor V. Danilevsky, a Soviet historian of science, remarked that Lomonosov with his publications not only antedated "Lavoisier by almost two decades and Mayer by a century," but also "saw immeasurably more than either of them." The Frenchman and the German each saw just one side of the basic principle, but "Lomonosov was the first to see both sides of this fundamental law of modern natural science." Danilevsky declared: "The law of the preservation of matter and energy must always and everywhere be called the Lomonosov law."

Less sweeping are other Russian claims for Lomonosov as the founder of the entire concept and practice of physical chemistry. Two centuries after Lomonosov, in an address delivered at the Soviet Academy of Sciences on November 17, 1961, Dr. Peter Kapitsa declared, "The modern reader is astounded by the fact that Lomonosov had a perfectly clear idea of the kinetic nature of heat. Lomonosov graphically connected the warming up of a body with the increase in the forward motion and the gyration of atoms and molecules, which were given by him other names, of course. Lomonosov developed these advanced ideas with an extraordinary consistency and logic. He came face to face, for example, with the concept of the absolute zero." Yet, Dr. Kapitsa also noted "Lomonosov's greatest mistake in one of the most fundamental problems of physics" when for a time, until 1757, he tried to oppose Newton's views and findings on the relation between the mass of a body and its weight; but after 1757 he did seem to recognize his error.

The Russians also point to Lomonosov's experiments and theories on electricity. These, they say, were sound, advanced, and radically different from the research and conclusions preceding his work. Then, too, they praise him for his inventions of wind-measuring instruments; of a thermometer that could record its work automatically if lifted into the upper strata of the atmosphere; of a spyglass that could be used in twilight and even at night.

Not too convincingly, they claim that his model of "an aerodynamic machine" was a worthy predecessor of the helicopter. As demonstrated to his fellow academicians in 1754, Lomonosov's little box contained thermometers and other small meteorological instruments. Although equipped with two pairs of wings and a watch spring, it rose only a short distance, and the little machine was abandoned.

The Russians say that Lomonosov's research into the properties of gases enabled him to establish the laws of ventilation in mines and that his experiments in chemistry helped his improvements in the technology of making stained glass. They hail him for his unerring mapping of a northeastern passage through the Arctic from Europe and Asia to America. His astronomical observations of 1761 proved, to his satisfaction, that there was indeed an atmosphere around the planet Venus.

The age of the sputniks that dawned in 1957 should make the world more aware of the scientist from Arkhangelsk, and Soviet science writers promise that it will.

In November 1961, in the Moscow *Tekhnika—molodezhi* ("Technology for the Young"), a staff member of the Soviet Institute of Physical Chemistry called Mikhail Lomonosov "Our Great Contemporary"; for, the writer proclaimed, Lomonosov does live with us in this wondrous space age. The writer invited his readers to imagine the day, which he said was not too far in the future, when a Soviet spaceship would approach the planet Venus and the cosmonaut's voice would reach all of us on Earth, announcing, "There is an atmosphere on Venus. Lomonosov was right."

IV

Alexander Pushkin wrote about Mikhail Lomonosov, "He founded our first university. To be more exact, he himself was our first university."

Yet Lomonosov neither left enough of a mark on the world community and cause of science nor, for a long time, was sufficiently appreciated even in his own country. Why so? In Dr. Kapitsa's November 1961 speech at the Academy of Sciences in Moscow we find the answer:

> In his work in physics and chemistry, Lomonosov was practically alone. To know the latest in science he had to consult literature, which at that time was quite scarce. He had no personal contact with the era's prominent scientists, since Lomonosov ceased traveling to foreign lands after his student days, and foreign scholars did not come to visit him in St. Petersburg, inasmuch as the Academy of Sciences of the time was not worthwhile. . . . The tragedy of the isolation from the world's science suffered by Lomonosov and other solitary scientists of Russia stemmed solely from the fact that they could not join the collective work of foreign scientists. This, then, is the answer to the question, "Why the lack of their work's influence upon the world's science?"

As for the lack of recognition at home in Russia, Dr. Kapitsa had this explanation: "For a scientist to achieve recognition it is necessary for the society surrounding him to be at a level high enough to understand and appreciate the essence of his work. Neither the administrative, official personnel nor the courtiers around Lomonosov could of course comprehend the significance of his scientific work. Therefore recognition of his work in physics and chemistry became possible only when our country had gained a scientific community all her own." In his own time "Lomonosov could not put to work the full strength of his genius. He painfully reacted to the absence of understanding and recognition for his work in his own country as well as abroad. Never did he derive that complete happiness from his creativity to which the might of his genius fully entitled him."

Pushkin in the early part of the nineteenth century was but a lone voice raised in praise of Lomonosov, that one-man university of the century before. Even at home, it was only in the twentieth century that fellow Russians began to be fully cognizant and amply proud of the great pioneer who had done so much and paid the price of his aloneness.

2. NIKOLAI LOBACHEVSKY
Non-Euclidean Pathfinder

THE greatest geometrician since Euclid was a Russian. His name was Nikolai Ivanovich Lobachevsky. Born on December 1, 1792, in the Upper Volga city of Nizhny Novgorod (now called Gorky), he lived and worked all his life on the shores of that river. The Volga city of Kazan and its university were his beloved milieu. He died in Kazan on February 24, 1856.

Bold pioneer of non-Euclidean geometry, he was at first censured by his superiors for daring to question theories hallowed by two thousand years of their acceptance as complete and infallible. His scholarly arguments were neglected by most of his colleagues in his lifetime; but Lobachevsky persisted, and finally won, even if he did not live to see his own victory.

For a long time before Lobachevsky, mathematicians had tried to deduce Euclid's fifth postulate—the postulate of parallel lines—from other postulates of Euclid. No one was able to deduce the fifth postulate from the others, despite a strong feeling on the part of geometricians that the fifth postulate was not independent of the other postulates. Lobachevsky was the first, however, to announce publicly that the fifth postulate was actually independent of the

Nikolai Ivanovich Lobachevsky. *Sovfoto*

others. Indeed, his demonstration of the independence required him to exhibit a geometry—which is called a non-Euclidean geometry—in which all of the Euclidean postulates, save the fifth, are satisfied; instead of Euclid's fifth postulate—to the effect that one and only one line can be drawn through a given point parallel to a given line—Lobachevsky's geometry has an infinite number of "parallels" through the given point.

Lobachevsky's concept, in its subsequent mathematical development, has been compared to the revolution wrought by Copernicus in astronomy. Aside from its impact on mathematics, Lobachevsky's ideas had a deep effect on philosophy and science, particularly near the end of the nineteenth century. For example, it brought about a significant change in theoretical physics in that the methods of regarding space were radically altered. This, in turn, paved the way, along with the experiments concerning the velocity of light, for the famous theory of relativity, which is couched in the language of non-Euclidean geometry.

II

Ivan Lobachevsky, the father of the genius, was a petty official in a government land-surveying office. There was little money in the family, but a good education for the children was available at the state's expense. When Nikolai was nine, his mother took him and his two brothers to Kazan, where they were boarded and taught in the ghimnaziya as wards of the government. It was a very good school, and the mathematics teacher, one G. I. Kartashevsky, was outstanding.

Entering the ghimnaziya in 1802, Nikolai stayed there until 1807, when, not quite fifteen, he was transferred to the University of Kazan. He was fortunate here again, finding four gifted and interested German professors: Johann Bartels and Kaspar Renner in mathematics, Joseph Littrow in astronomy, and F. X. Bronner in physics.

Native talent was still not too plentiful in Russia's grove of academe. In 1809, at the University of Kazan, although eight subjects were taught in Russian, nine were offered in foreign languages (five in Latin, three in French, and one in German).

Books in any language were few: on joining the faculty in 1810, Littrow complained that he could not find a single volume in the university library to be used as his students' textbook. Because the faculty and the facilities were increasing at a slow pace, the university was not in full operation until 1814.

But Lobachevsky was happy with the four Germans, particularly with Bartels in pure mathematics. Profoundly impressed with the horizons now opened before him, he soon abandoned his initial thoughts of a medical career. He would be a mathematician, and in this science he did astonishingly well from the very beginning. Professor Alexander Vucinich in his *Science in Russian Culture* (Stanford University Press, 1963) doubts that Lobachevsky would have created his new geometry if not for the stimulation he received from his four German professors, who, among other foreign newcomers, "re-established the avenues of Russia's scientific contact with the West." He learned from them, above all, a deep regard for rigorous logic with which to prove or disprove age-old premises.

Yet pleased as Nikolai's superiors were with his academic successes, they were dismayed by his unruly conduct. He took French leave on more than one occasion, running off to visit friends in the city, to make merry at a masquerade, and to indulge in various pranks. One evening in 1808, the university was startled by the sound of an explosion in the yard of the compound. A rocket went up into the sky, and it was Lobachevsky who had made it. His punishment was a period of incarceration in the university's *kartser*.

Lobachevsky was graduated from the university in 1811 when not yet nineteen. According to the custom of the time, the best of the graduates were awarded the degree of Master of Arts and Sciences and given positions on the staff of the university. Lobachevsky's name was high on this list, but his conduct was described in the official record not too glowingly: "In the last three years Lobachevsky was mostly of a very poor behavior, his transgressions being quite remarkable, setting poor examples for his classmates, but his frequent punishment not always correcting him. In his character he turned out to be stubborn, unrepentant, often insubordinate, and too self-centered, which led to many false illusions about himself." At one point, there was even a charge that he was inclined toward atheism.

No wonder, then, that his name was stricken from the roster of those to be rewarded on graduation. He was saved by his professors, who defended him before the administrators. He was given his master's degree and a minor assistantship on the university staff as a teacher of geometry to certain government officials. In 1814, at twenty-two, he began his regular university lecturing; and in 1816, at the age of twenty-four, he was first raised to professorial rank.

Bad times came for Russian universities in 1817 when Czar Alexander I, growing increasingly mystical and morose, established a unified Ministry of Church Affairs and National Enlightenment. For each of the few universities in the nation, special supervisors were appointed to root out whatever was considered too liberal or progressive. Kazan drew Mikhail Magnitsky, a notorious retrograde, who, on arriving in 1819, at once dismissed nine of the best professors. In 1820, Magnitsky recommended to the czar that the University of Kazan, being a subversive source of original thought, be abolished altogether. Fortunately, the czar demurred. Instead, stern instructions were dispatched that the Bible and the Prophets be the bases of the university's history and philosophy courses. Plaques with biblical quotations were installed in lecture halls.

Those professors who were not fired received these directives: "The professor of theoretical and experimental physics must throughout the duration of his course praise God's wisdom and the limitation of our feelings and means to understand the miracles surrounding us. The professor of natural history is to demonstrate that the great realm of nature is but a feeble reflection of that higher order for which we are destined after our short lives on earth."

A professor teaching mechanics at Kazan had to begin his course by declaring, "Our ancestor Adam received the instruction he needed directly from his Maker. He did not have to study the way we do, with so much labor and effort. He was an excellent theologian, philosopher, mathematician, naturalist, and so forth. Residing in that paradise in the East, he obtained light directly from the Sun of Truth."

One of Lobachevsky's fellow mathematicians on the faculty was convinced that the sole mission of mathematics was to prove God's presence in this world. He evolved a mathematical system that, he claimed, proved the main principles of morality as well as divine truths. He was happy to comply with the official dictum to be relayed to his students that in geometry the triangle was a symbol of the Father, the Son, and the Holy Ghost.

Lobachevsky's teaching was rather more sober. As Magnitsky's rule lasted seven years, Lobachevsky's position was in delicate balance. Until 1826, when Magnitsky was finally transferred (for reasons of corruption and other irregularities, which became too evident), there was his special surveillance over Lobachevsky's daily life and teaching; yet he recognized this professor's enormous ability and industry and not only allowed him to remain on the staff but even continued to promote him. The workhorse of the university, Lobachevsky had to substitute for several of his dismissed colleagues. He taught physics, mathematics, astronomy, and geodesy. He was ordered to reorganize the university library. He was dean of the faculty of physics and mathematics, beginning in 1820, when he was twenty-eight. The year after Magnitsky's departure, he became rector (president) of the University of Kazan. This was in 1827, when he was thirty-five years old. He ran the university for nearly two decades, until 1846, when he was forced to retire.

During the last thirteen years of his rectorship, matters were particularly rough; for although Magnitsky was gone, there was in St. Petersburg, from 1833 on, the evil chieftaincy of Count Sergei Uvarov, the reactionary minister of education under Czar Nicholas I, whose orders to repress enlightenment were valid everywhere, certainly including Europe's easternmost university, over which Lobachevsky presided.

III

Lobachevsky was thirty-one when, in 1823, he prepared his first geometry textbook, trying, among other things, to "prove" Euclid's fifth postulate. His superiors sent it for review to Academician Nicholas Fuss, a scientist imported to Russia from Switzerland back in 1773. Outraged by the young mathematician's presumption to "improve" upon Euclid, the old Swiss criticized the manuscript severely. As one of his points, Fuss objected to Lobachevsky's use of the meter instead of a more traditional unit of measurement; in this, Fuss saw the baneful influence of the French Revolution. This was practically the last scholarly act of the seventy-year-old Fuss: having penned his objection to Lobachevsky's ideas, he died in the same year of 1825—the significant year of the first unsuccessful uprising of Russian liberals against czarism, the so-called Decembrist revolt.

Lobachevsky was told to correct his text. This he refused to do; he did not even bother to reclaim the manuscript. There is a strong possibility that he was himself dissatisfied with it, particularly with his attempt to prove the fifth postulate. The manuscript was, for a long time, considered lost. It was found in the archives of some Kazan educational officials only in 1898 and was published in 1909.

This, by no means, represented Lobachevsky's only and last attempt to publish, and gain recognition for, his researches. Of course, he would not give up. Already by February 1826 he had completed in French his *Concise Statement of the Principles of Geometry, Together with a Rigorous Demonstration of the Theory of Parallels* (the original title was *Exposition succincte des principes de la géométrie avec une démonstration rigoureuse du théorème des parallèles*). That month, at a session of the mathematicians and physicists of the University of Kazan, he announced this work and made a brief explanation of its contents. He offered the full text of the *Concise Statement* to the discerning attention of his colleagues for their consideration and the text's possible publication in the learned journal of the faculty. Two professors and one assistant were given the task of review and decision. But all three showed utter disinterest in, or even scorn for, the work; and this manuscript was lost in the czarist archives irretrievably. One biographer guesses that the manuscript may have eventually been returned to Lobachevsky and lost by him. But we do have this comment by Lobachevsky himself, written nine years later in 1835, about his *Concise Statement* of 1826: "Vain attempts of two thousand years [to prove all of Euclid] compelled me to suspect that in his very concepts there was no such correctness as [scientists] endeavored to prove and which could be ascertained only by experiments, such as astronomical observations. Finally convinced of the justice of my hypothesis, and considering the difficult question solved entirely, I wrote my argument in 1826."

The argument of his *Concise Statement* was a sharp departure from his attempts of 1823. Now, in 1826, he left Euclid and for the first time advanced into his non-Euclidean realm—the "imaginary geometry," as he called it.

One year later, in 1827, Lobachevsky began the highest and longest phase of his administrative career as rector of the University of Kazan. From then on, he could at least publish his theories, if not garner applause for them. Indeed, in 1829–1830 his *Principles of Geometry* finally appeared in *Kazansky viestnik* or "Herald of Kazan," which was the university's own journal. One-third of this work was, in fact, based on his *Concise Statement* of 1826. This was followed by *Imaginary Geometry* of 1835; *Application of Imaginary Geometry to Some Integrals* (1836); *Geometrische Untersuchungen zur Theorie der Parallellinien* (1835–1838); and, finally, a grand summary of his life's work, *Pangeometry*, published in 1855, the year before his death. Of nongeometric works, there were his *Algebra or Calculation of Finite Series* (1834) and *Convergence of Infinite Series* (1841). In English we have an 1891 translation of his German text, *Geometrical Investigations on the Theory of Parallels.*

Lobachevsky was the first and most daring, but not the only, mathematician of his era to question or supplement Euclid, at least in part. Some non-Euclidean geometry, although not as well-developed as Lobachevsky's, was presented by the Hungarian mathematician Janos (Johann) Bolyai in 1832. Lobachevsky and Bolyai lived and worked unaware of each other. But Lobachevsky and Karl Friedrich Gauss, the world-famous German mathematician and astronomer, knew of each other. Lobachevsky's early German teacher Bartels had once taught Gauss when the latter was a twelve-year-old prodigy; Bartels may have been the first to tell Lobachevsky of Gauss's non-Euclidean interests. Indeed, Gauss had at one time sketched out certain premises of non-Euclidean geometry, and these pages were found among his papers after his death in 1855. But while he was alive he would not make his arguments public. Moreover, those of his disciples or colleagues who wondered about Euclid's total verity or clarity were severely discouraged by Gauss from any such speculation, experimentation, and publication. He frankly said he feared the traditionalists' outrage and outcry, but he admired Lobachevsky for his findings and his courage. In late November 1846, in a letter published only after the death of both Gauss and Lobachevsky, the German praised the Russian for his contributions offered "with masterly skill in the true geometrical spirit."

Part of the reason why Lobachevsky's writings and publications had to wait such a long time for their recognition was his heavy style. He made his complex reasoning yet more difficult to follow because he often wrote obtusely, if not obscurely. Even the friendly Gauss in humorous despair compared Lobachevsky's writings with "a confused forest through which it is difficult to find a passage and a perspective, without having first gotten acquainted with all the trees individually." An intellectual monthly in St. Petersburg published an unsigned derisive attack on Lobachevsky and his studies. Yet, already in 1842, there was some public evidence that at least some learned men understood and appreciated Lobachevsky. At home, a Kazan professor of mechanics, P. I. Kotelnikov, praised in print Lobachevsky's non-Euclidean researches and conclusions. Abroad, on Gauss's recommendation, the Goettingen Scientific Society elected him to membership.

IV

Although in his lifetime he remained (in the phrase of Professor Vucinich) this "poorly recognized titan" of geometry, but is now widely revered as one of humanity's greatest mathematicians, the situation is reversed with regard to his fame as a professional educator. In this latter role, he was well known while alive, but is barely remembered today.

Yet there is no disputing Lobachevsky's historic achievement in reorganizing the University of Kazan into a first-rank institution. Finding it a mere appendix to a middle school, he elevated it into its historic prominence, enriching its library and adding and improving its laboratories, but first of all appointing and promoting a superior personnel. He obtained specimens for the university's museums, instruments for its observatory, and books for its library. He originated a learned journal in Kazan that soon gained nationwide renown. As new buildings went up for the expanding school, he studied architecture to understand and help here too. The grace and solidity of the university halls were ascribed to his noble taste. He displayed personal bravery in addition to his administrative talent in saving the university's men and equipment in the cholera epidemic of 1830 and the catastrophic fire of 1842.

Undaunted by the repressive spirit of the era of Nicholas I, Lobachevsky early and late stated his enlightened ideas on education. In 1828, as the university's new rector, he spoke out in a major address on education as the main source of honor and glory of modern society. Education was to be all-inclusive: "Nothing should be eliminated, everything must be perfected." The intellectual capacities and emotional needs of youth should be both developed and served. Public schooling should be preferred to private tutoring—here was a daringly democratic voice.

He pleaded with students to lessen their interest in the Faculty of Law (which to the young men of the time was the surest way to good civil service jobs) and instead to consider the importance of the natural sciences. At all times, he praised science and scientific inquiry. Mathematics was, of course, the subject of his constant praise. The physical and mathematical sciences were to him "the triumph of the human mind."

But he also favored mankind's languages and literatures, and here he proved to be a unique innovator: he made a most significant contribution by enhancing the University of Kazan as a major Russian center of Oriental studies.

Here was a location and a tradition worthy of such use. This ancient Volga city, until the 1550s and its conquest by Czar Ivan the Terrible, had been the capital of the Kazan Tatar khanate. Tatar inhabitants were still in the majority in the nineteenth century; Tatar culture was preserved despite the Russian influx and domination. Lobachevsky had already found at the university a chair of the Arabic and Persian languages. To this he now added a chair of the Turkic and Tatar languages; and, later, that of the Mongol language and literature. Still later, studies of the Chinese, Armenian, and Sanskrit languages were introduced. Toward the end of his career, Lobachevsky planned to establish a chair of the Tibetan language. The Russian Orthodox Church was eager to use all this: missionaries were trained here to be sent into the Trans-Volga and Siberian regions of yellow and brown-skinned subjects of the czar. The Peking mission of the czar's church was staffed with graduates of these Kazan courses. Laymen, too, came to imbibe Eastern lore: in

1844, at sixteen, young Leo Tolstoy passed at the University of Kazan his examinations in elementary Arabic and Turko-Tatar. He wanted to be a diplomat and so entered the Department of Oriental Languages. But he soon found out that this was not to be his natural calling. He spent a rather indifferent academic year, 1844–1845, at the university, and withdrew.

It is on record that Lobachevsky and Tolstoy met and knew each other during these mid-1840s. At their first acquaintance Lobachevsky was fifty-one years old, Tolstoy not yet sixteen. It may be natural to suppose that Tolstoy would have been awed by the older man's wisdom and fame, and Lobachevsky would have been rather indifferent to, if not actually disdainful of, young Tolstoy, the aristocratic dandy who was then so neglectful of his studies that on one occasion he was even penalized by confinement in the university's kartser. And yet the two attitudes were actually in reverse: Tolstoy had no special admiration for Lobachevsky, while Lobachevsky appeared to discern much promise in the lazy youth. In his old age Tolstoy was to reminisce:

> What Lobachevsky had by then achieved in mathematics I at the time neither understood nor knew, but in his capacity as the university's rector he was attentive and friendly. His attitude toward me was very good. When, leaving the university, I had to pay him a parting visit, he most warmly expressed his regret that my university studies had not worked out. He said he would indeed be sorry if my outstanding gifts did not find a proper application. In just what he could then see my gifts, I really don't know.

Soon thereafter, in 1846, Lobachevsky was to terminate his long and successful career at the University of Kazan. This came very much against his will. He was in his mid-fifties and still in the prime of his strength when he fell victim to administrative intrigue. His superiors, taking advantage of a czarist law that decreed a professor's resignation after thirty years of service, deprived him not only of his teaching post but also of his rectorship. He was given what looked like a compensating position in the administrative hierarchy of the Kazan School District, but was, in reality, a demotion. He was regarded by many as a failure and a queer visionary, almost an eccentric.

The last ten years of his life and work, 1846–1856, were a misery.

He took the change in his post hard, as an unjustified affront, which in fact it was. To this was added the sharp misfortune of the premature death of his eldest son. There was much family illness; there were unexpected financial losses. He aged shockingly before his time. Soon he began to lose his sight. As he worked on his last book, *Pangeometry,* he could not write it—he had to dictate it.

Like Lomonosov, Lobachevsky left few, if any, early disciples. The magic of both was not in the classroom. They were to leave a far longer-range effect by their printed arguments and conclusions. Reverently, Dmitry Mendeleyev was to sum up: "Geometrical knowledge has formed the foundation of all the exact sciences, and the originality of Lobachevsky's geometry has marked the dawn of independent scientific development in Russia."

3. DMITRY MENDELEYEV
Father of the Periodic Table

FARTHER east, in the Siberian city of Tobolsk, on January 27, 1834, a child was born who was destined to follow Lomonosov and Lobachevsky as one more world-famous Russian scientist. This was Dmitry Ivanovich Mendeleyev, originator of the periodic system or table, which not only arranged the sixty-three chemical elements then known into a new and logical order, but also predicted the properties and places of, first, four more and, eventually, eight other elements then yet unknown.

In time, these were discovered, and still others in addition, until the total number of natural elements grew to ninety-two. In March 1969, on the one hundredth anniversary of Mendeleyev's epochal accomplishment, Dr. Glenn T. Seaborg, the American chemist and Nobel Prize laureate, wrote in the Soviet journal *Chemistry and Life:* "As the result of the phenomenally swift development of science in the last one hundred years, many generally recognized theories have become outdated. But Mendeleyev's periodic system to this day serves as the basis for subtlest and most complex researches. Therefore Mendeleyev's name will in the future, too, continue to be eternalized by new and yet newer discoveries of synthesized elements and by unlocking of new and yet newer secrets of nature."

Modern chemistry indeed stems from Mendeleyev's discovery. Ultimately, chemists established that the symmetry of his famous table came from this important factor: the electron ring structures govern the chemical properties of nature's elements. This has helped them to modify and expand the original table a number of times. In addition to filling the gaps indicated by Mendeleyev and beyond the eventual ninety-two entries, latter-day chemists have been able to synthesize twelve more elements, all heavier than uranium, which is the heaviest-known natural element. Of this dozen, nine superheavy elements were discovered by Dr. Seaborg

Dmitry Mendeleyev. *Sovfoto*

and his co-workers. Two of the dozen have been named after Russians: mendelevium (No. 101) in honor of Mendeleyev; and kurchatovium (No. 104) to honor the late atomic scientist Igor Kurchatov. Work continues in several world-renowned laboratories, Russian, American, and other, to synthesize still newer additions to the celebrated table.

II

On both sides of his family, Dmitry Mendeleyev came from bright middle-class stock. His father Ivan was from a family of clergy in the Province of Tver, northwest of Moscow. Ivan Mendeleyev was first a horse trader; but, when still young, he forsook business for a teaching career. He enrolled in a pedagogical college in St. Petersburg and, on graduation, took a middle-school headship in Tobolsk. It was in that city that he met a native Siberian beauty, Maria Kornilyeva, from a merchant family of some culture. (Back in 1787 her father established the first Siberian printing press and in 1789 launched a newspaper.)

Fourteen children were the issue of the marriage of Ivan and Maria. The mother was forty-two when their last child, Dmitry, was born. Misfortune struck the family that year of 1834: the father went blind and had to resign on a small pension.

Such a large family could not live on the scant one thousand rubles a year; so Maria moved the brood to a village seventeen miles from Tobolsk. There she was the manager and, later, the owner of a small glassblowing shop formerly belonging to her father. In 1837 a glimmer of hope appeared when Ivan was taken to Moscow for an operation on his eyes, which proved successful. But he subsequently became ill with tuberculosis; and in 1847, when Dmitry was thirteen, his father died.

The blond boy was growing up in a rustic environment, amid peasants and craftsmen; and already then, in his roaming in the Siberian countryside, he was curious about wonders of nature in a seriously inquiring way. One of his sisters was married to Nikolai Basargin, an exiled Decembrist; and this lively and learned man noticed and encouraged the boy's interest in chemistry, physics, and astronomy. He helped Dmitry with his lessons, making them exciting and meaningful.

From the age of seven years on, Dmitry was back in Tobolsk, going to school much of each year, but returning to the village and the family for vacations. He was an excellent student in the Tobolsk ghimnaziya, of which his father used to be the principal. Dmitry was graduated from that school at fifteen, in 1849, and the next year he traveled to St. Petersburg to enroll in the Natural Science Division of the Physics and Mathematics Faculty of the Main Pedagogic Institute. At first, his studies were not too successful. Only later did he reach the top of his class. As his specialty, he chose chemistry, in which he was fortunate to have an inspiring teacher, Professor Alexander Voskresensky.

Hard study affected his health. He began spitting blood, and a warmer climate was decreed for him. He moved to Simferopol in the Crimea and then to a teacher's job in Odessa on the Black Sea. His health improved, he returned to St. Petersburg to complete his courses. He was graduated from the institute in 1855 with a gold medal. Transferring to the University of St. Petersburg, he wrote and successfully defended his master's thesis in 1856. The next year he had his first university teaching appointment, giving a course in organic chemistry. He was to be associated with the University of St. Petersburg for thirty-four years.

In 1859 the czarist government rewarded him with a study journey to Germany. In his modest flat at Heidelberg, he set up a laboratory, where he did his increasingly significant research in physical chemistry. His discovery of critical temperature points was one of the products of this research. Western chemists began to notice his work, particularly after his active participation in the international congress at Karlsruhe, at which a unified system of atomic weights and chemical formulae was established.

He returned to Russia in 1861. In this year he not only resumed his lectures at the University of St. Petersburg, but also published the first Russian textbook on organic chemistry. Honors followed: his book won the famous Demidov Prize of the Academy of Sciences; in 1864 he was promoted to a full professorship at the St. Petersburg Institute of Applied Technology; in 1865 he defended his doctoral dissertation and returned to the University of St. Petersburg to a yet higher professorial post. In 1868 he began work on his textbook *Principles of Chemistry*, and it was in the course of this research and writing that he made his discovery of the periodic law of chemical elements.

Preliminary investigations leading to this discovery had been begun by him when he was still a student. At twenty, in 1854, he studied the chemical ingredients of certain minerals and concentrated on the problem of isomorphism. This led him to doing research on relationship between natural groups of elements. His main point was that the chemical activity of elements depended on their atomic capacity. In 1869 he was ready with the first variant of his table of elements. In March of that year, at home and abroad, he made public his brief statement entitled "A Tentative System of Elements Based on Their Atomic Weight and Chemical Resemblance." In the summer of 1871 he perfected his findings in his book *The Periodic Inevitability for Chemical Elements*. In his classic *Principles of Chemistry* (1869–1871), since that time republished in many languages, Mendeleyev for the first time presented inorganic chemistry on the basis of his periodic law.

III

Originally, while working on his periodic system, he had it arranged on cards, first on his desk, later on the wall of his laboratory—white bits of cardboard with symbols and weights on them and with gaps for the yet undiscovered elements here and there in the harmonious rows. Walter Sullivan, the well-known science writer for *The New York Times*, described the famous table on its centenary in March 1969:

> The construction of the table can be likened to the task of a hotel clerk placing letters in a bank of mail boxes, each of which is numbered. The letters are colored and numbered. They must be placed in the boxes in numerical sequence, starting in the upper left corner and moving horizontally across each row.
>
> The clerk is allowed to skip some boxes and to start a new row whenever he sees fit. If he succeeds, as did Mendeleyev, he finds on completing the job that all the blue letters are in one vertical column of boxes, all the red letters are in another vertical column, and so forth.

Периоды	Ряды	I	II	III	IV	V	VI	VII	VIII	0
I	1	1. H Водород 1.008								2. He Гелий 4.003
II	2	3. Li Литий 6.40	4. Be Бериллий 9.02	5. B Бор 10.82	6. C Углерод 12.010	7. N Азот 14.008	8. O Кислород 16.000	9. F Фтор 19.00		10. Ne Неон 20.183
III	3	11. Na Натрий 22.997	12. Mg Магний 24.32	13. Al Алюминий 26.97	14. Si Кремний 28.06	15. P Фосфор 30.98	16. S Сера 32.06	17. Cl Хлор 35.457		18. Ar Аргон 39.944
IV	4	19. K Калий 39.096	20. Ca Кальций 40.08	21. Sc Скандий 45.10	22. Ti Титан 47.90	23. V Ванадий 50.95	24. Cr Хром 52.01	25. Mn Марганец 54.93	26. Fe Железо 55.85 27. Co Кобальт 58.94 28. Ni Никель 58.69	
	5	29. Cu Медь 63.57	30. Zn Цинк 65.38	31. Ga Галлий 69.72	32. Ge Германий 72.60	33. As Мышьяк 74.91	34. Se Селен 78.96	35. Br Бром 79.916		36. Kr Криптон 83.7
V	6	37. Rb Рубидий 85.48	38. Sr Стронций 87.63	39. Y Иттрий 88.92	40. Zr Цирконий 91.22	41. Nb Ниобий 92.91	42. Mo Молибден 95.95	43. Ma Мазурий —	44. Ru Рутений 101.7 45. Rh Родий 102.91 46. Pd Палладий 106.7	
	7	47. Ag Серебро 107.88	48. Cd Кадмий 112.41	49. In Индий 114.76	50. Sn Олово 118.70	51. Sb Сурьма 121.76	52. Te Теллур 127.61	53. J Иод 126.92		54. Xe Ксенон 131.3
VI	8	55. Cs Цезий 132.91	56. Ba Барий 137.36	57. La * Лантан 138.92	72. Hf Гафний 178.6	73. Ta Тантал 180.88	74. W Вольфрам 183.92	75. Re Рений 186.31	76. Os Осмий 190.2 77. Ir Иридий 193.1 78. Pt Платина 195.23	
	9	79. Au Золото 197.2	80. Hg Ртуть 200.61	81. Tl Таллий 204.39	82. Pb Свинец 207.21	83. Bi Висмут 209.00	84. Po Полоний 210	85. —		86. Rn Радон 222
VII	10	87. —	88. Ra Радий 226.05	89. Ac Актиний 227	90. Th Торий 232.12	91. Pa Протактиний 231	92. U Уран 238.07			

Высшие солеобразующие окислы
R_2O | RO | R_2O_3 | RO_2 | R_2O_5 | RO_3 | R_2O_7 | RO_4

Высшие водородные соединения
RH_4 | RH_3 | RH_2 | RH

* Лантаниды

58. Ce Церий 140.13	59. Pr Празеодим 140.92	60. Nd Неодим 144.27	61. —	62. Sm Самарий 150.43	63. Eu Европий 152.0	64. Gd Гадолиний 156.9
65. Tb Тербий 159.2	66. Dy Диспрозий 162.46	67. Ho Гольмий 164.94	68. Er Эрбий 167.2	69. Tu Тулий 169.4	70. Yb Иттербий 173.04	71. Cp Кассиопей 174.99

An early copy of Mendeleyev's Periodic Table of the Elements. *Tass from Sovfoto*

Because letters of the same color—that is, elements with similar characteristics—recur periodically in this arrangement, the result is known as the periodic table of elements.

Until Mendeleyev, scientists limited their work to grouping elements by their chemical affinity, but did not research deeply enough into the inner connections of elements, particularly as concerned the dependence of their chemical and physical essence on their atomic weight. This is where Mendeleyev entered. He placed the sixty-three elements then known into his "periodic system"; and in the process he established that the separate groups, ascertained by other scientists earlier, now joined his system in a harmonious and logical whole.

Not that Dmitry Mendeleyev was the very first scientist to notice a certain recurrence or periodicity in the elements. Three years earlier, in 1866, a twenty-eight-year-old British chemist, John Alexander Newlands, made a public report in London about his discovery of what he called "the Law of Octaves" in the order of nature's elements. Like Mendeleyev, Newlands listed the elements in the ascending sequence of their atomic weight. Similar to Mendeleyev's findings, the conclusion reached by Newlands was that there existed a certain repetition of characteristics: he showed that every eighth element resembled the element that occurred eight places lower or higher on his scale. Mistakenly, however, Newlands connected this feature to the recurrence of octaves in music; hence, the name he gave to his discovery. He was generally too empiric in his approach; he did not thoroughly check the chemical characteristics of many elements as given by certain earlier, unscientific researchers. This led him to liken to each other such dissimilar elements as carbon and mercury or chlorine and nickel. His errors were so evident that he was widely derided from the start, one scientist in his audience asking sarcastically, "Why not list the elements alphabetically, and say that this is the natural system?"

Mendeleyev was far more painstaking; he took nothing on faith. He determined the properties of each known element through his own researches, and in so doing he set right some age-old mistakes. Typically, he corrected the atomic weight of nine elements, among them beryllium, indium, uranium, thorium, and cerium.

He was ready to present his findings on March 18, 1869, at a session of the Russian Chemical Society, newly formed in St. Petersburg. But he fell ill on the eve of the momentous day; and a friend, another chemist, unrolled the chart and made the statement for Mendeleyev. Shortly after, the discovery was made public in print and by letter to the entire scientific community of the world.

There were a few skeptical responses, but the general acceptance was early and strong. It grew steadily, particularly when, in the next fifteen years, three of the elements predicted by Mendeleyev—gallium, scandium, and germanium—were indeed discovered by West European scientists. In England, Newlands tried to dispute Mendeleyev's priority in the triumph, but his claim was patently weak and therefore disregarded. Mendeleyev's name became firmly attached to this great milestone in science.

In later years Mendeleyev was often asked just how he had made his astonishing discovery of the periodic system of elements. His answers were at times somewhat different. To a Czech chemist and admirer, Bohuslav Brauner, he replied, "When I first started writing my main textbook I felt that I lacked an order in which to distribute nature's chemical elements. I examined the scientific systems then existing for this purpose, and found all of them artificial. For my work I needed a natural system. I put down the signs of the known elements on small cards, noting their atomic weights in each case. I began to shuffle these cards this way and that, but no grouping satisfied me until it occurred to me to distribute them by their atomic weights, from the lightest to the heaviest."

But to a colleague at the University of St. Petersburg, the geologist Alexander Inostrantsev, he reminisced that the discovery had not been sudden at all; yet, at the end, quite dramatic. According to this account, for a long time Mendeleyev had suspected some sort of logical connection between elements. He had pondered this problem for months and years. Finally, there came weeks of intensive thinking and scribbling; he "spoiled a lot of paper in the effort to compose a table that would prove some kind of law, but to no avail." The climax, according to the geologist quoting the famous chemist's reminiscence, came in the following way.

One time Mendeleyev stayed up all night long in trying to devise the right table. The search being as ever fruitless, Mendeleyev with a heavy heart stopped his work. Tired and sleepy, he dropped onto a sofa in his study and, without undressing, fell asleep. That morning he saw a dream. The dream was precisely and clearly the table that later brought him worldwide fame. He was overjoyed even in his sleep. In fact, so strong was his joy that it awakened him and drove him back to his desk, where he quickly jotted down what he had just seen in his dreaming.

In 1959, the Soviet chemist Academician Ilya Chernyayev wrote:

A cursory glance at Mendeleyev's life and work may produce an impression that he always scattered himself as he researched problems of dissimilar branches of science. But this was not so. The great chemist devoted thirty-eight years to his work on the periodic law. And he displayed the very same persistence and consistence as he worked on all those other problems. Mendeleyev was a systematic genius, who possessed the rarest quality of mind to see order in everything and to apply the laws of this order in everything. As he researched most disparate problems of science, Mendeleyev related to them his own principles of nature study, always remaining a most original and a most profound thinker, able to tackle successfully even such scientific problems which at that time appeared insoluble.

IV

The range of Mendeleyev's interests and researches was indeed amazingly wide. He dealt with fluids extensively—their viscosity, thermal expansion, and capillarity. He worked in meteorology and metrology. He was a pioneer in agricultural chemistry. He gave time, thought, and toil to various industrial processes, among them the manufacture of smokeless gunpowder. He designed a differential barometer. He did much work on the present and the future of Russia's oil and coal resources. On August 7, 1887, he ascended in a balloon to study the total sun eclipse of that day. Four years later he gave a hand in preparing a new tariff that would protect and strengthen Russian industries. He wrote much and profoundly on the riches and the destiny of the Russian nation. For occasional relaxation, he did some bookbinding and suitcase-building, achieving a level of rare professionalism in both hobbies. (There was a story about the chemist concerning his visit to a store to buy materials for one more suitcase: A bystander, impressed by the flowing beard and general imposing appearance of Mendeleyev, asked the shopkeeper, "And who is that man?" The merchant was astonished. "What, you don't know? Why, that is Dmitry Mendeleyev, the famous suitcase maker!")

Five Russian universities elected him an honorary member of their faculties. On his journeys to Western Europe and America, all doors were wide open to him. Cambridge, Oxford, and other prestigious universities and learned societies bestowed honors upon him. In his lifetime Mendeleyev received more than one hundred doctorates, medals, and other signs of recognition in eleven countries.

Yet amid all this applause, Mendeleyev's path was not always smooth. Unbelievable though this may sound, the majority of the Imperial Academy of Sciences in St. Petersburg refused to accept him in 1874, and again in 1880, when some of the nation's foremost savants proposed his candidacy. The secondary rank of "correspond-

ing member" was the best that was given him (1876). In 1890 he had
to leave his post at the University of St. Petersburg as the result of
his conflict with the czar's minister of education, which arose from
Mendeleyev's temerity in delivering to that functionary a petition
from some rebellious students.

Still, such was the patriarchal inconsistency of the czarist government that soon after depriving him of his post at the University of
St. Petersburg, it used him as an economic consultant in the blue-
printing of the new tariff (1891) and appointed him as head of the
Imperial Bureau of Standards and Measures (1892).

As for his personal life, he was not altogether happy in his first
marriage. He was married, without love, almost absentmindedly, in
1863, when he was twenty-nine to a Siberian woman a few years
older than himself. They had children and in later years coexisted
rather than cohabited, peacefully, until the spring of 1877, when a
seventeen-year-old girl entered the life of this world-famous scientist aged forty-three.

She was a Don Cossack girl, Anna Popova, a lively student of art
and music, a friend of one of his nieces. So lovelorn and ill did
Mendeleyev become that he could no longer go on with his
researches. He was listless as he lectured; he lost all interest in life.
Alarmed, his colleagues sent delegations to plead with his wife to
release him to his young lady, for the good of Russia's science, as it
were. It took more than four tense years for the romance to resolve
happily—for Mendeleyev's wife finally to agree to a divorce. In
January 1882, Dmitry and Anna were married, he at forty-eight, she
at not quite twenty-two. Of the children of this second marriage,
daughter Lyubov grew up to marry the celebrated Russian poet
Alexander Blok, while son Vasily became a naval and military engineer who as early as 1911 presented a design of a tank with a
cannon, a machine gun, and a crew of eight soldiers.

V

Dmitry Mendeleyev lived long enough to see the Russian Revolution of 1905–1906 and its failure. He died early in 1907 at the age of
seventy-three.

In the summer of 1906, only a few months before his death, he completed his last book. Its subject was not chemistry. Entitled *Toward an Understanding of Russia*, the volume was the scientist's last will and testament on the problems of geography, demography, economics, and politics. Mendeleyev examined the map and the natural resources of the Russia he knew and projected his nation into the future. On the basis of the time's population figures and his people's birthrate, he predicted 282,700,000 inhabitants for the Russian Empire of 1950. He was, as we now know, too optimistic. He did not foresee the losses wrought by the two world wars, the Soviet revolution, and the terror and starvation in the wake of the latter, which were to cost Russia so many millions of lives.

But already then, amid the revolutionary rehearsals of 1905–1906, Mendeleyev sensed what damage could be caused by excesses of socialistic-communistic totalitarianism. In his final book he warned against such excesses. He advocated man's free labor as a means of modernizing his country in contrast to "the error of the basic premises of Communists and Socialists." With astounding clarity he saw the inevitable and harmful emergence of a large and powerful bureaucracy if and when a communistic regime would take over. He wrote: "Should, God forbid, utopias of Socialists and Communists anywhere and in any guise be established, the number of just those who would allot work, and force people to do such work, and supervise the workers and the general order of things, would exceed many, many times the number of our era's 'functionaries.'"

Mendeleyev wanted his nation to grow and expand northward and eastward, to and through the beloved Siberia of his origin and of the many untapped resources. He wanted Russia to come closer to China and be an intermediary for peace between China and the West. He wished neither wars nor revolutions, but peaceful life and harmonious toil everywhere.

Such was the great scientist's parting message to the mankind he loved and enriched with his genius.

4. ILYA MECHNIKOV
Seeker and Healer of Life

THE foremost Russian scientist to seek the root and riddle of life was Ilya Ilyich Mechnikov. He was one of the world's founders of evolutionary embryology and comparative pathology. He came forward with solutions to complex problems of microbiology and immunology, and for this work was awarded the Nobel Prize in 1908 (he was Russia's second scientist to become a Nobel laureate; Ivan Pavlov, the physiologist, was first in 1904).

Several years after Mechnikov's death, Sir Ray Lankester, a British colleague and friend, wrote truly of the Russian's pioneering—of Mechnikov's observations and theories, so independent and so decisively original as to make him "a solitary figure contending, and successfully contending, during the best years of his lifetime for the recognition of a great generalization for long opposed by most of the medical and physiological authorities of the time, and finally established by his lifelong researches and those of his faithful pupils and coadjutors." A Russian associate, Dr. Nikolai Gamaleia, who lived to be ninety, looked back at his work with Mechnikov and saw him as few could see the legendary savant: "Decades will pass and men will conquer cancer, leprosy, and many other diseases which now are considered incurable. And people will always remember with grati-tude the hallowed name of Ilya Mechnikov, the great Russian naturalist who so brilliantly began the campaign for human health."

Mechnikov started his adult life as a restless seeker and an irate pessimist. He ended it as a man in his early seventies who had finally found some of the reassuring answers that we human beings need. True, as he lay dying, the horrors of the First World War were raging around him, seemingly negating his optimism. But the hope he discovered in his later years lived on despite the bloody habits of foolish mankind. You can find that hope not alone in the many shelves of the learned biological and medical works Mech-nikov wrote, but also in the heritage of such of his philosophical books as *The Nature of Man*, *Studies in Optimism*, and *Forty Years' Search for a Rational Outlook*.

II

Mechnikov was born on May 15, 1845, in a village in the Ukraine, Province of Kharkov, the last of five children, the son and namesake of a nobleman of rather moderate circumstances who, nevertheless, had a houseful of serfs to cater to every need and whim of the Mechnikov family.

Many years later, Ilya Ilyich Mechnikov's widow, Olga, wrote that "his ancestors on both sides included talented individuals, from whom he may have inherited his gifts and his innate taste for science." On his father's side, he was a collateral descendant of Nikolai Milescu, better known as Spathary, a Moldavian nobleman of Greek ancestry, who was educated in Constantinople, and even-tually moved to Muscovy, where he served Czar Alexis and his son, Peter, as a scholar and a diplomat, most notably as the Russian envoy to China in the 1670s. Spathary married a Russian girl; the family—including some nephews who came out of Moldavia to join the original Spathary—became Russian. The name of one of the nephews, Mechnikov, was a translation of Spathary, which meant "sword-bearer."

On the maternal side, Ilya Ilyich was of Jewish origin. His moth-er, Emilia, was the daughter of Lev Nevakhovich, a wealthy and talented Jew of Warsaw, who, on an indirect suggestion from Czar

Ilya Mechnikov at work in his laboratory. *Sovfoto*

Alexander I, had himself and his family baptized into the Christian faith, becoming Lutheran and moving to St. Petersburg. His sons joined the Imperial Guards and led a rather empty life, but he himself translated German philosophic treatises and revolved in the capital's literary circles. His daughter, Emilia, a vivacious brunette with flashing dark eyes, inherited his intellectual tastes and abilities. Her friends called her "Milochka," which means "charming" or "darling." On meeting her at a ball, the great poet Alexander Pushkin, an acquaintance of her father, exclaimed: "How well your name suits you, Mademoiselle!"

The blond, blue-eyed Ilya Ivanovich Mechnikov—father of the future scientist—met the dark beauty through her brothers, his fellow guardsmen. Ilya and Emilia were married, and the guardsman proceeded to spend his young wife's dowry and inheritance. His passions were cards and horses. Finally lacking any further means to keep up such a life in St. Petersburg, he moved himself and his family to that moderate-sized Ukrainian estate. Before departure, Ilya Ivanovich secured a remounting job—buying horses for two regiments. This he did in the Ukraine between his two main occupations: entertaining relatives, friends, and neighbors at well-arranged and endless meals and running long sessions of cards.

The senior Mechnikov was not very successful at either managing the estate or influencing his children. The first job was taken over by a self-sacrificing younger brother. The second was done, most ably, by Emilia Lvovna, the strong personality in the Mechnikov menage. The scientist's widow, Olga, was to recall eventually that he "himself considered that he had inherited his mother's disposition and turn of mind." Above all, the father was not at all interested in the five children, but the mother was, intensely and rather intelligently. The children were quick to perceive the difference from their tenderest years on. Scientist Ilya felt close to his mother to the end of her life.

Of the four boys in the family, the eldest, Ivan, grew up to be a prominent lawyer. The second, Lev, was a geographer and a traveler who, while living abroad, became Giuseppe Garibaldi's friend and aide-de-camp. In one battle for Italy's independence, Lev was wounded, but recovered. The third, Nikolai, took after his father; his life was idle and not at all distinguished. The only girl in the family, Catherine, did not leave much of a mark either. The fifth child, Ilya, showed his great promise from the very beginning.

As a child, he was restless, inquisitive, and tenacious in whatever held his interest. Nature and its wonders absorbed him from an early age on. At eight, under the influence of a tutor, Ilya started a herbarium. At eleven he studied the life of a hydra. It was at eleven, in 1856, that he was taken from the family estate to the city of Kharkov to enter the high school. He studied all subjects well, read much and fruitfully, and made the honor roll easily. The Russian language teacher singled him out and helped him by suggesting books to read. Among these, Henry Thomas Buckle's *The History of Civilization in England* impressed the boy tremendously. By stressing that science was the foundation of true progress, the volume confirmed Ilya's choice.

A schoolmate came from the family of a paint manufacturer. The boy's elder brothers were studying chemistry at the University of Kharkov to help the family's business. Through the influence of this classmate and his brothers, Ilya's interest in the physical sciences grew ever more. He soon joined a group of high school students who distributed among themselves certain scientific fields for special study and for eventual reports and discussions with one another. Ilya was fifteen when, after reading a book entitled *Classes and Orders of the Animal Kingdom*, he decided to study the lowest of those orders—to learn all there was to know about life in its simplest form. At sixteen he had his first article published; and even before completing his high school courses, he attended lectures at the University of Kharkov. A young professor of physiology liked the eager youth and agreed to give him private lessons in histology.

Through his friends at school, Mechnikov became acquainted also with the radical publications of the era. He read forbidden journals, but his preoccupation with science was stronger. Moreover, a childhood memory of an attack by drunken peasants upon his family turned him against the thoughts of violence as a solution to mankind's sociopolitical ills. He would be a liberal, not a radical. And in the spirit of his time, he would be a scientist first and foremost.

The latter 1850s and early 1860s formed the epoch when Russia's young intellectuals were infatuated with the natural sciences. In his *History of Biology in Russia*, written in 1913, Mechnikov looked back a half century and summarized:

> Society was in a ferment and experienced a resurgence of mental activity. The scientific aspirations of secondary school pupils were encouraged, not suppressed by too strict demands on their classical education. Greek was absent from the curriculum and Latin was a mere formality of secondary importance. Their place was taken by natural sciences which attracted special attention of young people. The traditional lectures "according to the book" in universities were superseded by a livelier presentation of the subjects from scientific sources, and scientists working independently gradually began to make their appearance.

In 1862, at seventeen, graduating from the Kharkov high school with a gold medal, the school's highest final honor, Ilya became a college student, enrolling in the Natural Science Division of the Physics and Mathematics Faculty at the University of Kharkov. That fall he completed his first scientific work, "Some Facts from the Life of Infusoria." He was overjoyed when a naturalists' journal in Moscow accepted it, but soon was horrified to discover serious mistakes in the main argument of his essay and wrote to the Moscow editor not to publish it. To the end of his long life he was certain that the article was not printed—without realizing that the article was indeed published several years later in another magazine by an editor who had inherited it from the first editor without knowing that the author had recalled the piece as erroneous.

Ilya was nineteen when, in 1864, he completed the four-year university course in two. In later years he was somewhat regretful of this speed because he felt it had left certain gaps in his general education. But he did not think of this university and most of its curriculum and professors too highly. As a student he selected only a few subjects and yet fewer instructors, and concentrated with those. At all times in his life, he was an impatient individualist. Already as a youth he displayed certain qualities that were true of his lifelong character. With much justice, Professor Semyon Zalkind, a Soviet biographer, wrote of him in 1959: "Mechnikov was a theoretician attracted to general scientific problems, given to making broad philosophical generalizations, impetuous and quick in his conclusions, sometimes apt to disregard facts but self-confident and persistent in the attainment of his aims."

III

In 1864 Mechnikov came to the conclusion that he would find truer science abroad, and so he spent the next three years in Western Europe. He began with the island of Heligoland, where he did research on the Fabricia, an annulate worm, and where several German scientists paid benevolent attention to him, attracted by his youthful enthusiasm, solid knowledge, and imaginative ideas. From there he traveled to Giessen to a naturalists' congress, where he was among the youngest to deliver learned papers. He read two papers on his Heligoland researches and met still more able and admiring German scientists.

At first he lived on the little money his parents were able to give him. He strung it out by eating little and scrimping ingeniously. When he decided he must stay abroad longer, he applied to the St. Petersburg Ministry of Education for a subsidy, and this was granted since the scientific promise and performance of this precocious scientist were so evident.

Becoming absorbed in certain questions involving the worm type of the Nematodes, he obtained the permission of a celebrated German zoologist to work in his laboratory while that scientist was away on a vacation. He discovered in his researches that hermaphrodite and parasitic Nematodes gave birth to a free bisexual generation. He presented the proof of his discovery to the German scientist on the latter's return. His host was quite annoyed that such results had been achieved in his laboratory during his absence. He proposed that the young Russian and he continue this work together. Later, while Ilya was away, the German published the findings as his own, not even as a collaboration. Ilya was furious, but there was no redress. In the words of his wife, Olga, he soon found that "kindliness was rare between colleagues" in Germany; yet he did continue to have much respect for "the great capacity for work of the scientists of that country; he admired the organization of their laboratories, allowing every force, great or small, to be utilized and making useful collective work possible in those complicated researches which demand the collaboration of divers specialists."

Mechnikov lived and researched in Italy and Switzerland. Together with a young Russian scientist, Alexander Kovalevsky, whose close friend he became, he contributed to the foundation of comparative embryology. Both were early advocates of the Darwinian theory of evolution. Following the embryological researches of a German scientist, Fritz Mueller, who proved Darwinian principles on certain crustaceans, young Mechnikov added his share in finding the key to animal evolution in the most primitive stages of life that he chose to study.

While abroad, he also found time to read the latest philosophical works. Through his brother Lev, in Geneva, he met the famous Russian radical exile Alexander Herzen. Later in Italy, the fiery anarchist Mikhail Bakunin was a friend and a frequent companion of his. He was fond of both Herzen and Bakunin without agreeing with their politics, and this may have been known to czarist spies. At any rate, his acquaintance with these and other Russian radicals in Western exile did not appear to hurt Mechnikov's academic career when he returned to Russia.

He wrote his thesis and was awarded his degree as a Master of Science in 1867. In that year he was also appointed assistant professor at the Novorossiyisky University in Odessa. He was twenty-two; he lectured to third-year students, many of whom were older than himself, but who were much impressed with both his erudition and his liveliness. But he soon ran into trouble with his elders and superiors on the faculty. He wanted to be his university's delegate to a naturalists' congress convened in St. Petersburg in late 1867, an honor coveted by an older professor. An argument ensued, and Mechnikov rather unjudiciously told his students about it. They hooted at the older contender publicly. The unpleasantness was settled when both were sent to the congress.

Mechnikov's participation in the sessions was a success. Many scientists in the capital had already known of him; a number made friends with him. The result was that he was offered a professorship in zoology at the University of St. Petersburg. He spent some time researching in Italy, then came back to Russia to assume his new post. In 1868 he wrote and defended his doctoral dissertation at the University of St. Petersburg. Like his master's thesis, this also summarized his researches in embryology.

But his new life and work in the resplendent and exciting Russian capital belied his fond hopes. By then his eyes were affected by his continuous work with the microscope. He never had enough money and did not seem to manage taking care of his everyday needs. To increase his income, he took on a lectureship at the School of Mines. He had to walk to this work long distances in cold weather. These particular students interested him but little. He was discouraged; irritated; and, most of all, lonely.

He decided to marry. He resolved to find a paragon of a wife, a young woman who would be handsome and demure, intelligent and tender, devoted to his needs both at home and in the laboratory—in short, an all-around loving mate and assistant. He conceived a plan of finding an unspoiled girl and bringing her up carefully, aye, scientifically, to his specifications.

He thought he found such a girl in the family of Andrei Beketov, a professor of botany and rector of the University of St. Petersburg. Ilya fell ill; and, being all alone and uncared-for in his lodgings, he was taken by the Beketovs to their house to recover. His friends had a daughter, a girl of only thirteen. Ilya thought this was just the right age. He would train the unspoiled miss to love him, and as she grew up, he would create the wife he wanted. But soon he was puzzled and hurt: the girl was "perfectly indifferent to me," he wrote to his mother in the fall of 1868. "So my fond plans went awry. I was much upset by this, because, next to my scientific work, this undertaking was closest to my heart."

Presently, he was consoled by the discovery that the Beketovs had a niece, closer to his age and eager to link her fate with his. He was practical enough to write to his mother that for Lyudmila Fedorovich he had "a strong affection" rather than any overwhelming love. "I shall not try to assure you," he added, "that we shall live the rest of our days together as two turtledoves. I am far from imagining our distant future as enveloped in a kind of rosy haze."

He knew that Lyudmila was of frail health, but late in 1868 he nevertheless married her. The time appointed for the ceremony happened to be one of her bad lapses; yet the young couple would not postpone the wedding; and so Lyudmila was carried into the church in a chair.

What had been thought to be a mere persistent bronchitis turned out to be tuberculosis. The young wife needed a city warmer than St. Petersburg. Mechnikov's old competitor at the Odessa University having retired, an offer of a professorship of zoology and comparative anatomy seemed attractive. Mechnikov accepted it in 1870 because that city in the south would be good for Lyudmila's health. But she grew worse and worse. Taking time off from his university duties, borrowing money, obtaining research subsidies, he took Lyudmila to balmy parts of Western Europe. At times she seemed to improve, but not for long. After slightly more than four years of this miserable marriage, in the spring of 1873, on the island of Madeira, Lyudmila Mechnikova died. Burying her on the island, Ilya returned to the continent.

Stopping in Geneva, he decided on suicide. By his later reminiscence, he said to himself at the time: "Why live? My private life is ended; my eyes are going; when I am blind I can no longer work, then why live?" He took morphia, but in such a large quantity that he at once vomited all of the poison out of his system.

Recovering, he still thought it would be best to end it all. Yet, one night, as in despair he was walking across the Rhone bridge, he saw a cloud of insects around a lamp. At a distance, he took them for Ephemeridae; and he forgot about killing himself, intrigued by the sudden question, "How can the theory of natural selection be applied to these insects? They do not feed and only live a few hours. They are, therefore, not subject to the struggle for existence. They do not have time to adapt themselves to surrounding conditions." On coming closer, he saw these were not Ephemeridae, but Phryganeidae; but the question about Ephemeridae persisted.

His interest in science, and thus in his own life, revived. He went back to Russia full of new and vigorous plans.

IV

Mechnikov returned to Odessa and its university. The preceding years, despite his family problems, had been fruitful: between 1865 and 1869 he had completed some thirty treatises on the development of such minute kinds of life as the Suctoria, tapeworms, Nemertinea, Rotifera, ringworms, Turbellaria, Gastrotricha, Mollusca, insects, and the lowest of the Chordata. From 1869 to 1874 he continued to study these forms and added to them the Crustacea. Dr. Zalkind summarized this phase in Mechnikov's work: "This provided new embryologic proof of the unity of the entire animal kingdom." The conclusion to be drawn from it was: "Germ layers are homologous in all multicellular animals, since they are similar with respect to their position and role in the processes of organogenesis."

Yet toward the end of this period, right after Lyudmila's death, Mechnikov continued to be weak and shaken. His eyes still bothered him; and so, on his return to Odessa, he devoted most of his effort to lecturing instead of to the microscope. He took time out to travel east to the Kalmuck steppes for some anthropological researches, which, however, did not prove to be of much value. When in the summer of 1874 he came back from the second of these trips, he found himself living in an Odessa house whose upper story was occupied by the family of a prosperous landowner. The eldest child was a girl of sixteen. The lonesome scientist, now nearing the age of thirty, once more thought of his old idea of educating a malleable young female to be his perfect wife.

Ilya Mechnikov and Olga Belokopytova were married in February 1875, he still a few months short of thirty, she seventeen. In the church, during the ceremony, people were heard to whisper, "Why, she is a mere child!" Triumphant, Ilya carried Olga off to set up a new household and to help her prepare for her final examinations at the high school.

They were destined to have a long and happy life together, marred only by a few occasional disagreements and, at that, in the early part of their union mostly. Art was Olga's main preoccupation. She drew and painted well, but she also had a bent for the natural sciences, and under his tutelage she proved to be a capable laboratory assistant. She shared his interests completely; she forgave his outbursts of temper and even one more attempt at suicide in 1881. Curiously, the shock of this attempt and the consequent recovery seemed to cure his eye trouble for good. He returned to his microscope with ease and joy, and had no ocular difficulties the rest of his life.

In her biography of her husband, Olga Mechnikova was extremely reticent on the subject of having children; but apparently she gave in to Ilya on this. She wrote: "He harbored pessimistic theories to that extent that he looked upon the procreation of other lives as a crime on the part of a conscious being." But as the years advanced, his pessimistic spells gave way to zest for life and general optimism; and his temper tantrums disappeared entirely. Still, the Mechnikovs had no children, even though Ilya was exceptionally tender to the children of his relatives and to his several godchildren.

Mechnikov's second stay at the Odessa university lasted twelve years, from 1870 to 1882. Already the years from 1875 on were marked by the governmental onslaughts upon academic freedom. Measures against freethinking professors and students were being taken. Mechnikov, a liberal and a scientist, tried to stay out of national politics; but university politics could not be ignored. Quick-tempered, outspoken, he defended progress against repression. The assassination of Czar Alexander II by the revolutionaries in March 1881 in St. Petersburg set off stringent reactionary steps by the government of the new sovereign, Alexander III, throughout the empire. The effect was felt in Odessa as well. Boiling with ire, Mechnikov handed in his resignation. It was at once accepted.

The Mechnikovs were not destitute, however. Olga's parents died at that time, within a year of each other. She and Ilya inherited a big share of the Belokopytov estates in the Ukraine, as well as the guardianship of her two brothers and three sisters. In the fall of 1882, using the income of the estates, the Mechnikovs and the children settled in Messina, Italy.

V

It was during his intense researches in the Straits of Messina that, by Mechnikov's own testimony, "the great event of my life took place: a zoologist until then, I suddenly became a pathologist." He was at that time studying intracellular digestion of the lower animals and the origin of the intestine. From such simple experiments his thought and work progressed to the similarity of these phenomena to the formation of pus, of inflammation in man and other higher animals. Olga later summarized his reasoning as follows: "In man, microbes are usually the cause which provokes inflammation; therefore it is against those intruders that the mobile mesodermic cells have to strive. These mobile cells must destroy the microbes by digesting them. Inflammation is thus a *curative reaction* of the organism, and morbid symptoms are no other than the signs of the struggle between the mesodermic cells and the microbes."

Mechnikov called his discovery *phagocytes*, a word that is the Greek for "devouring cells." He published his first essay on his theory in a learned journal in Vienna in 1883. It at once aroused the skepticism and opposition of a number of scientists, particularly in Germany. Years passed before enough proof came forth to substantiate these findings by Mechnikov.

The Mechnikovs tried settling down in Russia once more in 1886, when Ilya accepted the appointment as scientific director of the newly established Bacteriological Institute in Odessa. The chief sponsors of the institute were the municipality of Odessa and the *zemstvo* (regional council) of the Kherson Province. Some of the medical staff of the institute had had their preliminary training in antirabies inoculation at Louis Pasteur's institute in Paris.

At the Odessa institute, Mechnikov did research on the microbes of erysipelas and of relapsing fever and directed the staff in other studies and inoculations. One experiment was to infect cereal-destroying rodents of the southern steppes with chicken cholera. An ignorant St. Petersburg journalist launched a hostile campaign in his mistaken belief that chicken cholera could turn into Asiatic cholera. On other issues, local Odessa physicians opposed Mechnikov, chiefly because he had no specific medical education. Mechnikov went from dismay to disgust to despair. He and Olga left for a trip to Western Europe, for a breath of fresh air, as it were. They would look around for a better place for life and work than Russia could then offer.

The year was 1887. For a while, as they traveled and talked to foreign colleagues, they thought of some quiet German university and laboratory. This search in vain, they finally reached Paris; and Mechnikov called on Pasteur. The great French scientist was then sixty-five and ill. Mechnikov described their first meeting:

> On arriving at the laboratory for preventive antirabies vaccination, I saw an old man wearing a black skull-cap covering his close-cropped greying head, short of stature and partially paralyzed, with penetrating grey eyes, a grey moustache and a beard. His unhealthy, pale complexion and tired appearance told me that the man before me had not long to live—perhaps only a few months.
>
> Pasteur received me very cordially and at once began to discuss the topic closest to my heart—the problem of the body's fight against microbes. He said: "I at once placed myself on your side, for I have for many years been struck by the struggle between the divers micro-organisms which I have had occasion to observe. I believe you are on the right road."

Highly pleased, Mechnikov rather timidly asked Pasteur for a chance to work by his side. Pasteur was just then planning a new and bigger building for his institute. He offered Mechnikov not just a place in a laboratory, but a whole new laboratory and a headship over it.

The Mechnikovs went back to Odessa to wind up their affairs. In the spring of 1888 Ilya handed in his resignation, and in the fall he and Olga pulled up their stakes in Russia for the last time. On October 15, 1888, he began his service at the Pasteur Institute.

Pasteur died in 1895. Mechnikov stayed on as director of the institute until his own death, a total of twenty-eight years, the happiest part of his life. "Thus it was in Paris," he later wrote, "that I succeeded in practicing pure science apart from all politics. That dream could not have been realized in Russia because of obstacles from above, from below, and from all sides. One might think that the hour of science in Russia has not yet struck. I do not believe that. I think, on the contrary, that scientific work is indispensable to Russia, and I wish from my heart that future conditions may become more favorable."

Ilya and Olga were destined to return to Russia several times, but on visits, not to settle there again. In 1897 Ilya traveled to Moscow to read two papers at an international scientific congress, one on the phagocytic reaction against toxins, the other on the bubonic plague. Both were outstanding successes. But the real triumph was the Mechnikovs' visit to Russia in 1909, when they came to their native land en route from Sweden after Ilya had received his Nobel Prize. In St. Petersburg and Moscow, excited throngs of scientists, students, journalists and others flocked to banquets, learned sessions, and other gatherings at which Mechnikov was honored. The trip was crowned by a day spent at Yasnaya Poliana with Leo Tolstoy and his family in great warmth and deep philosophic discussion. Two years later, in 1911, Mechnikov headed an elaborate expedition organized by the Pasteur Institute to study tuberculosis among the Kalmucks of eastern Russia. This turned out to be an occasion on which not only Russia's intellectuals but even her czarist officials made a point of applauding the great scientist.

In St. Petersburg, the Academy of Sciences did not repeat the error it had committed in the case of Mendeleyev. Ilya Mechnikov was elected the academy's corresponding member in 1883 and its full member in 1902. Other honors, from the academies, learned societies, and universities of the entire world flowed to Mechnikov in an incessant stream. Biologists and physicians, young and not so young, asked for the privilege of studying and researching under Mechnikov at the Pasteur Institute; and he opened the doors widely. Russian visitors and researchers were numerous among the polyglot brotherhood presided over by Mechnikov in Paris, as new and yet newer lifesaving vaccines emerged to the eagerly waiting world.

VI

Once his phagocyte theory was established, Mechnikov moved from the study of inflammation to his researches on the rise in body temperature as another pathological phenomenon. As he increasingly busied himself with immunology, he experimented with cholera, syphilis, and other infectious diseases. In 1892 he and several of his associates deliberately infected themselves with cholera, the better to study its effect, its cure or prevention. It was for his work in phagocytosis and immunology that in 1908 he was awarded the Nobel Prize (sharing it with Paul Ehrlich, the German scientist who so brilliantly did research on toxins and antitoxins, especially in the treatment of syphilis).

Gradually, as he grew old, Mechnikov became engrossed in problems of aging and death. As a bacteriologist par excellence, he riveted his attention on man's large intestine. He pointed to it as an excessive reservoir of food and thus of bacteria. The shorter the intestine in a living being, the fewer microbes it contains, and the longer is the animal's relative span of life. Man's large intestine as a storehouse of food was very useful to his animal ancestors in their struggle for survival, for it allowed them to flee from their enemies for a long time and distance without stopping for their bodily functions. But now this storehouse is one of refuse; it is man's nemesis. Since the large intestine cannot be artificially shortened, at least the microbes in it can be reduced in numbers and virulence.

Mechnikov began to experiment with diet. Sir Ray Lankester reminisced that while treating his guests to excellent wine and cigars, Mechnikov himself neither drank alcohol nor smoked any tobacco whatsoever. "He was very careful about the possible contamination of uncooked food by bacteria and the eggs of parasitic worms, and in consequence had rolls sent to him from the bakers each in its separate paper bag, whilst he would never eat uncooked salads or fruit which could not be rendered safe by peeling. This was not an excess of caution, but resulted from his characteristic determination to carry out in practice the directions given by definite scientific knowledge, and to make the attempt to lead so far as possible a life free from disease."

His preoccupation with sour milk as the best food possible became world-famous. On learning that in Bulgaria and other Balkan countries many people lived to advanced ages and that they ate quantities of fermented milk, particularly in the form of yogurt, Mechnikov investigated this milk scientifically and came to a tentative conclusion that therein lay the secret of man's longevity.

Bacteria in curdled milk were benevolent; they fought other—bad —bacteria. Around the year 1900 he experimented with varieties of milk fermentation and finally came upon a recipe that became the mainstay of his diet.

Nevertheless, as he neared the age of seventy, Mechnikov ailed increasingly. It was, however, his heart, not his stomach and intestine, that gave him trouble. Just before Christmas of 1913 he wrote: "At the ages of 50, 60, 65, I felt an intense joy in living, such as I described in my *The Nature of Man* and *Studies in Optimism*. In the last few years it has lessened markedly. Scientific work still provokes in me an invincible enthusiasm, but I am becoming more indifferent to many of the pleasures of life." On May 16, 1914, he wrote: "I have today entered my seventieth year; it is a great event for me. As I analyze my feelings, I realize more and more the *weakening* of my 'life instinct.'"

The outbreak of the war late that summer was a grave blow. The tumult and the brutality of the conflict overwhelmed Mechnikov. The work of his beloved Pasteur Institute was disrupted. Many young doctors and research associates marched off to the hostilities, and soon there was word of deaths on the battlefield of some of them.

For many years the Mechnikovs had led a happy existence at their country home in Sèvres, from which Ilya used to commute to his Paris laboratory. But now, owing to the war and the increasing difficulties resulting from it, they moved to the city, to the Pasteur Institute, where they occupied a small suite. In the summer of 1916, as Ilya's illness worsened, they were given Louis Pasteur's own old apartment. It was here that Mechnikov fought his last contest with death.

The life instinct proved strong at the end. He who in his younger years twice tried to commit suicide, who risked his life by inoculating himself with cholera, now—at seventy-one—did not want to die.

But on July 15, 1916, he died. He was cremated, and the ashes were brought back to the Pasteur Institute, there to stay in a place of honor. The day after his death, Maxim Gorky, the Russian writer, in a letter to a scientist in Petrograd (formerly St. Petersburg) urged him to tell the Russian people "how much it has lost by the passing of this man—about his precious optimism, about his profound understanding of the value of life and his fight for it."

By far the greater part of Mechnikov's life, work, and achievements occurred outside his native country, in a kind of deliberate self-exile. Many Russians felt this keenly; yet they refused to take it as a slur on Russia. They chose to view Mechnikov as Russia's son and pride, who in spirit had never left his fatherland. For a long time afterwards, they remembered the words with which Academician Ivan Pavlov, his fellow Nobel laureate, greeted Mechnikov on his visit in St. Petersburg in 1909: "A tremendous Russian scientific force, recognized by the whole world."

5. IVAN PAVLOV
Genius of Conditioned Reflexes

A Soviet biographer has called Ivan Petrovich Pavlov "the world's greatest physiologist." A Soviet encyclopedia hails him as "the creator of the materialistic science of the higher nervous activity of animals and man." This is the closest the official Soviet doctrine could bring Pavlov to being a Communist and an atheist, neither one of which the great scientist was, of course. But the Communists did try to use Pavlov's findings about conditioned reflexes to justify and strengthen what they were doing. Pavlov objected and grumbled, but did accept the Soviet homage and did continue his work under the Communist regime; this was for him an alliance of convenience.

Pavlov's best biographer, Professor Boris P. Babkin, wrote his teacher's life after leaving Soviet Russia and was thus freed from any pressures except his own sincere admiration for the great master. More factually than Soviet writers, Babkin describes Pavlov as "the famous Russian physiologist," whose name "is familiar to every educated person." Pavlov himself, sixteen and one-half months before his death, evaluated his accomplishments as, in part at least, due to a celebrated Russian predecessor, Ivan M. Sechenov, "and an army of my dear co-workers." All this combined effort, Pavlov wrote on October 14, 1934, "subjected the whole animal organism to the mighty power of physiological investigation," and the result was "entirely our Russian achievement and a contribution to world science and human thought."

Russia old and new has been immensely proud of this compatriot who, back in 1904, was the first Russian scientist to be awarded the Nobel Prize. One of the longest-lived Russian savants, Pavlov was in his eighty-seventh year when he died. He headed the celebrated Institute of Experimental Medicine for forty-five years of his astonishingly fruitful life. From 1902 till his death in 1936, he devoted thirty-four years to the study of the cerebral cortex by the method of conditioned reflexes, which he was the first to introduce with so much meaning and success. In the words of Dr. Babkin, "Pavlov regarded his work on conditioned reflexes as his greatest scientific achievement, and it was truly his beloved child."

II

Pavlov was born on September 26, 1849, in the ancient Central Russian city of Ryazan. On both sides, he came from families of clergy. Ivan was the first child and eldest son of Peter and Varvara Pavlov. Peter's father—Ivan's grandfather—was a village sexton. Peter, on graduating from a seminary, received one of the poorest town parishes in Ryazan, but steadily advanced until at his life's end he was among the most distinguished priests of that city at the head of one of its best parishes.

Reading and gardening were high on the list of Father Peter's spare-time occupations, and this love was early communicated to his son Ivan. Even as a young poor priest who had to economize in everything, Father Peter bought books, and not on theology alone. Because he came by them at such sacrifice, and because of his deep respect for learning, the priest read every book at least twice, and told his son to do the same—"to understand it better." Little Ivan followed this advice solemnly and carried it into his adult life, just as for years and decades to come, with passion and skill, he toiled in vegetable patches, fruit orchards, and flower gardens whenever he could find free time from his researches and lectures.

Yet because of the early struggle, Pavlov's father trembled over each ruble and kopeck even after reaching prosperity. He was extremely reluctant, almost stingy, about helping his son as a struggling student and young penniless scientist at a time when Ivan and his wife and children needed this aid desperately.

But this was to be in the future. Meanwhile, as a child, Ivan Pavlov was growing up sturdy and happy, excelling in such vigorous pastimes as *gorodki*, a folk game of skittles. Then came misfortune: at the age of nine he fell off a fence to a brick floor. His lungs seemed to have been injured. Two years of serious illness followed. At one time, he appeared on the point of death. But the boy's godfather, an abbot of Spartan habits, took the boy to his monastery near Ryazan; and here, through a sensible regimen of fresh air, good food, and much exercise, he restored Ivan to health and returned him to his family in the city. The memory of the abbot remained a lifelong influence with the future scientist. He was particularly impressed with the godfather's self-demanding habit of constant, steady work. All his life he would work just as assiduously.

Because of the illness, Ivan's formal schooling was delayed. It was only at eleven that he was enrolled in the Ryazan Ecclesiastic High School. The year was 1860, the bright dawn of the great reforms undertaken by the young Czar Alexander II in the wake of the long reactionary reign of his late father, Nicholas I. The new spirit liberalized even the teaching methods and the entire atmosphere in the clergy's high schools of Russia. But this novel freedom was felt with an especial force in the Ryazan Theological Seminary, to which Ivan and his two brothers, Dmitry and Peter, transferred after graduating from the high school.

Professor Babkin, in his excellent biography of the great scientist, writes of Pavlov's seminary years: "Many of the teachers at the seminary were very young people, who experienced the uplift of the sixties." Their methods were extremely liberal. "They were free from that pedantry with which instruction was permeated in the classical schools even in my time, that is, in the nineties of the past century. The seminary was interested not in the average pupil who was obliged to succeed in all subjects but in the individual capacities and inclinations of each boy. If a boy distinguished himself by knowledge of or devotion to some one subject, they overlooked his shortcomings in other subjects." Ivan certainly profited from this approach; for in the middle of his seminary studies, he became irresistibly drawn to the natural sciences.

In the freedom-loving 1860s, liberal and even radical literature was being read and passionately discussed by the Ryazan seminarians and the younger of their teachers. Foremost among the fiery publicists of the time in his influence upon Russian students and other intellectuals was Dmitry Pisarev, a nobleman in his twenties, who wrote prolifically on the problems of individual ethics, on literature, on women and the family, all in tear-it-down terms of no moderation or compromise. Arrested in 1862 at the age of twenty-two, Pisarev spent four and a half years in solitary confinement in the Peter-Paul Fortress, from which he kept up his flood of outspoken books and essays. On his release, he continued his activities until at twenty-eight in 1868 he perished in a drowning accident in the Baltic Sea.

Many Russian intellectuals became revolutionaries under the impact of such teachings as Pisarev's. At the time and in later years, Ivan Pavlov acknowledged his admiration for Pisarev, but the latter's effect on Pavlov turned out to be in a category all its own: because Pisarev denounced any and all studies except those of the natural sciences, because he proved the value of the natural sciences to mankind's progress so convincingly, Pavlov believed in and chose just such studies or at least was deeply confirmed in his initial belief and interest in such scholarship. It was from Pisarev's writings that Ivan Pavlov first learned, with enthusiasm, about Darwin's theory of evolution. But of Pisarev's atheism and radical politics, young Ivan accepted nothing. Already then, in the 1860s, and certainly in his later years, Ivan Pavlov was a deeply religious man and a political liberal, a man of constructive convictions, not a destroyer.

III

At this time the reform-minded government of Czar Alexander II saw fit to relax its regulations concerning theological seminaries: divinity students were allowed to give up their courses for lay education in universities. In 1870 Pavlov and two of his fellow seminarians took advantage of the dispensation. They traveled from

Ryazan to St. Petersburg, where they enrolled in the university's Faculty of Physics and Mathematics, Division of Natural Sciences. A year later, the younger Pavlov, Dmitry, joined the group.

Along his early way, Ivan Pavlov met a book and a professor. The book was *Reflexes of the Head Brain* by Ivan Sechenov, and it proved to be the very first impetus to Pavlov's interest in the cerebral cortex. But more immediately there was his acquaintance with Professor Ilya Tsion (called Cyon in Babkin's biography). This professor noticed and favored the student from Ryazan almost at once.

Under his guidance, in his celebrated laboratory, young Ivan carried out several research projects. For one of them, done in collaboration with another student, on the nerves of the pancreatic gland, Pavlov in 1875 was awarded a gold medal by the University of St. Petersburg. This work, however, prolonged his university course by one year. Graduating in 1875, he enrolled in the third year of the Medical-Surgical Academy, intending to add formal medical knowledge and a medical degree to his record. Professor Tsion had already moved from the university to the academy and had offered Ivan a highly valued assistantship in his new laboratory.

However, just then, Professor Tsion quit his post and left Russia altogether. Soviet historians, while paying due tribute to Ilya Tsion's brilliance and great contributions to physiology, explain that his students protested against his reactionary views in the politics of the day, and this was why Tsion was forced to leave. In reality, it was Tsion's aggressive and unpleasant personality, and more particularly his tough grading system (once, in 1874, he failed 130 students who were thus forced to repeat an entire year at the academy), rather than his ultraconservative politics, that led to his departure from the academy.

Be as it may, Tsion's resignation was a blow to Pavlov. Now he had no assistantship nor hardly any other means of existence in the capital. Another professor offered him an assistantship, but Pavlov doubted his honesty as a scientist and declined the offer.

Life was hard for the Pavlov brothers (Dmitry was studying chemistry, later to become an assistant to Mendeleyev) and their fellow students from Ryazan, with whom they roomed and shared their scant provisions. Oftentimes the whole group subsisted on tea and bread for days at a stretch; but when one of them received a food parcel from home, the feast was common. Tutoring, manuscript copying, and other such low-paying chores stole time from their lectures and laboratory sessions, but added the necessary pittance to their budget. Frequently, lacking streetcar fare, they walked to and from their pupils' homes or other bread-earning appointments long distances in the worst of St. Petersburg weather.

Meanwhile, Ivan Pavlov was turning into a first-rate scientist-experimenter. In 1876 he did obtain an assistantship in the Physiological Laboratory of the Veterinary Institute, and this he held until 1878. Having learned some of his techniques from Professor Tsion and adding his own inherent talent, he was soon known for the speed, dexterity, and precision of his experiments on animals; the bold initiative and revealing results of his projects on the operating table; and the clarity of his explanations to his student audiences. In this period he successfully conducted several independent investigations into the physiology of blood circulation and the physiology of digestion. In the summer of 1877 he scraped together enough funds to do research in Breslau, Germany. The result of this was his first published work, in 1878, on the effects of ligation of the pancreatic ducts in rabbits. In 1879 he published an account of a new operative procedure developed by him for making a permanent pancreatic fistula.

Already in 1878, still a student, he was invited by the famous Professor Sergei Botkin to head the academy's newly established laboratory of experimental physiology. Pavlov remained in charge here for ten years, at first learning from the gifted Botkin, then, in some respects, surpassing even that master of experiment and discovery. Pavlov's biographer Dr. Babkin writes: "The direction of this laboratory was intrusted altogether to Pavlov, since Botkin was overloaded with other responsibilities. This is in truth an amazing fact—that a recently graduated science student, who had not yet finished his medical course and who himself should have been studying under another, became the director of scientific investigations in the most famous clinic of internal diseases in Russia."

In December 1879, Pavlov was graduated from the Medical-Surgical Academy, receiving a gold medal for the impressive total of experimental work done by him as one of the school's most distinguished students. But it was not until 1883 that his doctoral dissertation was defended by him and the degree of Doctor of Medicine was given to him. From 1880 to 1884 he held a scholarship at the academy for postgraduate study and research. In 1885 and 1886 he spent two years on a governmental research scholarship in Western Europe.

He was by then a husband and father. In the spring of 1881 he had married a naval doctor's daughter, Serafima Karchevskaya, who had come from Rostov on the Don to study in the Pedagogical Institute of St. Petersburg. It proved to be a lifelong, happy union, although the first ten years or so were an excruciating time of economic hardship. The young wife was wont to complain that in his concern over and work on other students' projects in the laboratories he headed, Ivan neglected his own opportunities for promotion and better salary. On one occasion, she came to him with the news and lament that he had failed to receive a professorship concerning which both of them had been hopeful. She found him examining sorrowfully some dead cocoons. He listened to her, then said, "Oh, leave me alone, please. A real misfortune has occurred. All my butterflies have died, and you are worrying over some silly trifle."

Some of his students also worried about his lack of practical sense. They decided to alleviate his need by collecting money for him and then presenting it to him for a course of special lectures they would ask him to deliver for them. They were dismayed when he used the money to buy a pack of dogs for experiments.

IV

The Medical-Surgical Academy was renamed and reorganized as the Military-Medical Academy in 1881. Three years later, in 1884, Pavlov was appointed to its teaching staff as *privat-dotsent* (lecturer or assistant professor), but the salary was shamefully low. Things improved only in 1890, when he was promoted to the rank of professor of pharmacology. In 1895 he became the academy's professor of physiology, and he occupied this chair until 1925.

In 1891 he was also invited to become director of the Physiological Department at the Institute of Experimental Medicine, which was opened the year before. For many years he researched and taught at both the academy and the institute. He found the latter place more congenial and remained at the institute until his death forty-five years later. It was at the institute that, unhindered and increasingly respected, he did some of his best work on the digestive glands and conditioned reflexes. At the Military-Medical Academy, on the other hand, intrigue and petty politics were rife; and too much of Pavlov's time and effort was wasted by his strong-willed, irritated participation in this campus struggle unworthy of him.

Pavlov was an impatient, irascible man, demanding of his wife, family, and colleagues. He generally had his way. His selfishness and rudeness were usually forgiven. From early years on, it was recognized that he was a genius and that even his frequent selfishness served mankind, not him personally. His admiring biographer Dr. Babkin wrote:

> Pavlov served an ideal of the highest and noblest character. He firmly believed, until the end of his life, that only through science can humanity be made happy. He did not require much for himself; the simplest life . . . satisfied him completely. All those who lived and worked with him, including his wife, had to sacrifice their own interests for his, if they wanted to remain with him, for his own interests were not his personal interests in the strict sense of the word but lay outside him, so to speak.

The first period of Pavlov's scientific work, 1874–1888, was devoted primarily to research in the area of animal heart and blood vessels. His doctoral dissertation of 1883, *The Centrifugal Nerves of the Heart*, showed for the first time the existence, in a warm-blooded animal, of special nerve filaments increasing or diminishing the heart's action. Later, on the basis of his further researches, Pavlov proved that the nerve discovered by him affects the heart through a change in the metabolism of the heart muscle. In time this led to Pavlov's work and theories of the so-called trophic innervation. Already in his doctoral dissertation he had written: "The nervous system controls the greatest possible number of bodily activities."

Nevertheless, his outstanding early achievement, winning for him worldwide recognition, was his experimental physiological researches on the digestive glands. Pavlov pioneered in the systematic application of antiseptic and aseptic surgery in the study of the digestive glands and their functions. He produced brilliant results in his researches on the nervous regulation of the secretory activity of these glands. He came out with new findings of the functions and actions of gastric glands, the pancreatic gland, and the mammary gland and gradually—in 1901–1902—became more and more engrossed in the study of the animal's conditioned salivary reflexes.

Although the present-day layman associates Pavlov's name with the study of conditioned reflexes, the Nobel Prize of 1904 was awarded to him for this earlier work on the digestive glands. Even though at the time Russia was just entering the turbulent period of the Revolution of 1905, the man in the street—and surely the Russian intellectual—found time to be proud of its first scientist to be awarded the Nobel Prize. Pavlov himself tried to remain calm and even modest. He pretended to be annoyed by his wife's excitement at the news of the prize and admonished her in the words of the biblical commandment: "Thou shalt not make unto thee any graven image or any likeness of anything. Thou shalt not bow down to them nor serve them." He added, "There is nothing exceptional in my work; it is all based on facts from which logical conclusions were drawn. That's all."

In reality, of course, the laurels of revolutionary discoveries in physiology do belong to Pavlov. He proved the existence of enzymes of ferment in the gastric juices. He opened curtains to knowledge about man's higher nervous system. But his work on reflexes was indeed his crowning triumph.

V

It was in his famous experiments of many years with dogs that Pavlov uncovered conditional reflexes. Applying the stimuli of certain sounds to an animal before his intake of food, he established a conditioned reflex—a flow of saliva—which later he could and did provoke again by repeating the sound stimulus, but not giving the food expected. This led to other experiments and discoveries of yet wider ramifications by Pavlov and others in the fields of medicine, psychology, and other areas of modern science. Pavlov's researches on reflexes, both conditional and unconditional, proved truly a great divide in human progress.

He was elected a corresponding member of the Academy of Sciences in 1901 and a regular member only as late as 1907. Honors from the universities and learned societies and academies came to him in a constant flow from the world over. At home, material conditions for his continuing research improved to a point where in 1913 funds came for him to plan and build at the Institute of Experimental Medicine the so-called Tower of Silence—a special building with soundproof chambers, the better to study his beloved reflexes.

From time to time he traveled abroad, in his younger years to give his wife the pleasure she found in Italy, Switzerland, and other foreign lands; in later years to international conferences and congresses. He enjoyed meeting foreign scholars, particularly after he himself had become famous; but at all times he detested non-Russian landscapes, food, and customs and said so loudly, repeatedly, and most unreasonably.

His Russian patriotism was on the chauvinistic side; but it was one of the main reasons why, despite his violent disagreement with the Communists, he would not emigrate after the revolution together with the millions of other dissatisfied Russians.

Ivan Pavlov in 1934 working in his laboratory on his experiments in animal conditioning. *Sovfoto*

He stayed in his home and laboratory and continued to experiment and lecture, even in the worst times of terror and starvation. When electricity failed and there were neither kerosene nor candles, he operated on animals in the feeble light of *luchina*, the peasants' age-old oil-dipped splinter of wood. When food ran out, Pavlov expanded his lifelong habit of raising vegetables so as to have enough provisions not alone for his family but also for his staff.

The civil war over, the victorious Communists remembered the destitute scientists, particularly those who could be useful to them, such as Pavlov and his researches. Vladimir Lenin and his high council thought that here, in the Pavlovian methods of dealing with conditioned reflexes, was the beginning of a system through which they, the Communist overlords, could not only justify their regime but, most viably, also train the rebellious or reluctant masses to respond to certain cleverly devised stimuli.

And so in 1921 Lenin himself initiated and signed a decree calling for specially favorable conditions to be arranged for Pavlov and his work. Pavlov's materialism was to be equated with Communist materialism, and never mind the old scholar's eccentric insistence on churchgoing. Lenin's order was promptly carried out. The Soviet officials soon boasted that whereas before the Communist take-over, Pavlov had had only three assistants—one per each of his three laboratories—he now commanded a staff of fifty. In time, at Koltushi (now Pavlovo) near Leningrad, a spacious and well-equipped center for his experiments was built, which the great scientist in much delight called "this Capital of Conditioned Reflexes."

At the very beginning of the Soviet regime, it was fairly common for dissenting Russian intellectuals to make flip or tart remarks about Marx and Marxism. If they erred, it was on the side of caution; they indulged in this criticism of the new state religion in private only. Very few dared to air their opposition or doubts in public. The secret police were strong, and they showed no mercy.

Among the bold handful, Academician Ivan Pavlov at first spoke up with particular verve. At one point in the very beginning of the 1920s, he dared a political—anti-Communist—preface to an otherwise nonpolitical lecture, with which he opened a course he gave to Communist students in Moscow.

Then for at least ten years before his death in 1936, Pavlov said hardly anything political—at least, not in public. Not that he was afraid for himself; his worldwide fame was too powerful a deterrent even for Stalin's police to act against him. Most likely, he simply did not want to bother; and he was getting old and tired even if not afraid.

It is true that in the last four or five years of his life, Pavlov, on occasion, publicly did praise the Soviet government, but not for its basic ideas and practices, only for the concern and aid it extended to the cause of the nation's education and science. There was never a word of approval from him for any of the reactionary practices of the Communist regime, for its terror, for its suppression of freedom. To the end of his life Ivan Pavlov remained a moderate liberal.

He died on February 27, 1936. The last document that came from his pen was a letter to the youth of his country, a kind of final will and testament, particularly to those young who wished to dedicate themselves to science. He urged the virtue of consistency upon them—"consistency in storing up knowledge." Start at the very beginning, he said. "Never tackle that which follows without having acquired that which precedes. Never attempt to cover up gaps in your knowledge by guesses and hypotheses, no matter how bold. Train yourselves to be restrained and patient. Learn to do dirty work in science. Study, compare, store up facts."

Consistency, Pavlov wrote, should go hand in hand with modesty. "Never think that you already know everything," he warned. "And no matter how high the others' appraisal of you, have the courage to say to yourselves, 'I am ignorant.'" This will make you go on with your search for true knowledge, he promised in that remarkable document.

Above all, have passion for science: "Science demands of man a colossal determination and a great passion. Science asks of man his entire life. And even if you had two lives, still they would not be enough. So be passionate in your work, in your seeking."

6. KONSTANTIN TSIOLKOVSKY
Prophet of the Space Age

T HE back country beyond Ryazan, Ivan Pavlov's native city, gave Russia and the world yet another outstanding scientist who, however, was destined to gain far less recognition during his lifetime and after it than the great physiologist was afforded. This was the pioneer and pride of Russian rocketry, Konstantin Eduardovich Tsiolkovsky, born in 1857, dying in 1935.

He was a self-taught scientist of Russian-Polish-Tatar blood, picturesque yet obscure for many years even in his native land, but acclaimed in the fullest possible measure by the Soviets today, though still little appreciated outside Russia. Already in the 1880s and 1890s this provincial teacher of physics and mathematics sparked off some original ideas on sending rockets into outer space. It was he who evolved theoretically the multistage principle in rockets and the use of solar energy for some of the batteries in the artificial satellites of the future and who was, so the Russians insist, among the very first to diagram an earth satellite and a space platform.

Tsiolkovsky published his first important paper on rockets in

Konstantin Tsiolovsky in 1934. *Sovfoto*

1903; his second, in 1911. Because of these and other—earlier and later—works he is now proclaimed by the Soviets to have been years, nay, decades ahead of either German or American rocket pioneers. But Western experts today, although tending to concede to Tsiolkovsky more credit than formerly, still doubt that even chronologically, in the more crucial areas of his researches and speculations, he was really ahead of America's Robert H. Goddard. As Western astrophysicists reexamine Tsiolkovsky's papers, their judgement is that his thinking and writing lacked the rigor of either Goddard or Germany's Hermann Oberth.

It is true that deaf, poor, neglected as he was—and at times most naive—he tried to solve certain problems already answered and written up in the West. He did not consciously try to take for himself all that credit properly belonging to the Western researchers. It was simply that, isolated by poverty and insufficient communication, he did not know of their findings in time. Toward the end of his life, in 1928, he wrote: "I discovered much that had already been discovered before me. These discoveries are important to no one but myself, for they gave me confidence in my abilities."

There was progress even in such attempts to break down the doors that had already been unlocked. "At first I discovered old truths, then not so old, and finally quite new ones," he later summed up.

Recognition came slowly and in pitiful doses; yet it did come. Before he died, Tsiolkovsky saw his own Russian pupils and followers send up the first rocket of value to science.

Often and with much anger he denied that he devoted his life's work to creating an escape for humanity. Man should not leave the earth for good—he should stay on earth and improve his lot here. But man also must aspire to the universe: "Man has the right to penetrate the universe. We must thus enrich man's life!"

II

Konstantin, or Kostya for short, was born on September 17, 1857, in the village of Izhevskoye on the shore of a large lake of the same name, in the sleepy, woody province of Ryazan near Moscow.

His father Eduard, a Pole, was an underpaid forester and unsuccessful inventor. He loved to construct machinery and once, with his own hands, built a fair-sized thresher, which, however, failed to work. He led his sons in the construction of models of palaces and houses. He was also a homespun philosopher with an idea and a saying for practically every person met or event experienced. He was writing a vague philosophic opus, left unfinished and, of course, unpublished at his death. Often he was morose as well as restless.

Kostya's mother, Maria Yumasheva Tsiolkovskaya, was a gifted woman, cheerful and witty even in the face of the family's cruel want. She was a Russian, with an admixture of Tatar stock; she came from a clan of artisans, of peasant origin, low-class, but clever. "My father's main trait was force of character and will," Tsiolkovsky was to recall in later life. "My mother's—talent."

He was an energetic boy, climbing trees and fences, building huts of tree branches and twigs for his and his playmates' camping, flying kites with boxes containing cockroaches as passengers. At eight he received a much-appreciated gift from his mother: a small collodion balloon filled with hydrogen. He daydreamed that there was no gravity. He read voraciously and made up his own stories and even paid his younger brother for listening to his fancies.

At nine came his first misfortune. He weathered, with difficulty, a siege of scarlet fever. The result was that for the rest of his long life he was almost totally deaf.

Because of his deafness and for lack of an effective hearing aid, he lost his early friends; and he could not hear his teachers. He had to quit school. So already as a child he withdrew into himself and learned mostly by himself from the books he found in his father's library. He mastered first mathematics, then physics. At fourteen he made a tissue paper balloon, filling it with smoke. He built a small turner's lathe, which he used to construct and run a tiny carriage with a turbine inside.

Wings and winds absorbed him. On his makeshift lathe he built models of flying craft with flapping wings. They did not rise from the ground, but he was sure that someday they would. He spoke of someday building a large navigable balloon within a thin metal shell. Of this time Tsiolkovsky later wrote:

> I was fascinated by the astrolabe which enables us to measure distances to objects beyond our reach. I constructed a height-finder. Then, with the help of the astrolabe, I calculated the distance between our house and the fire tower without going outdoors. The calculation showed it to be 1,200 feet. I then measured the distance with the measuring rod and in this way verified my calculations. This made me believe in theory.

But a new blow came: Kostya's mother died when he was thirteen and so much in need of her. His father, more melancholy than ever, managed the large brood alone and poorly.

The father did try his best. Eduard watched his son with increasing awe. The boy should go on to higher education even if it meant another sacrifice in food and clothes for the rest of the family. So at sixteen, off to Moscow the youth went, with an allowance of ten to fifteen rubles a month, a stoic wrench for the other Tsiolkovskys.

III

Konstantin stayed in Moscow three years. There he went to libraries, not schools. He read much, mainly in physics and mathematics, keeping up with the official programs of the czarist secondary schools and universities of the early 1870s and going beyond them too.

He lived in slums and starved himself, spending most of his allowance on books, either those he could not find in the Moscow libraries readily or those he wanted to have by his bedside even at night for instant reference. He also bought quicksilver, sulfuric acid, and retorts for the experiments he tried out in his room. He purchased materials for his models and so would not spare any money even for potatoes or tea. In his autobiography he recalled: "I remember very well that I had nothing to eat but dark bread and water. I would go to a bakery once in three days and buy nine kopecks' worth of bread. In this way I spent on bread ninety kopecks a month. For all that, I was happy with my ideas, and my diet of dark bread did not dampen my spirits."

Konstantin barely noticed Moscow's color and bustle around him as he buried his bony face in volumes full of formulas, but he knew of every scientific lecture or debate open to the public, and he attended them with a beating heart and halted breath. He had fashioned for himself a crude but effective tin horn as a hearing aid; and once more, even if reservedly, he felt himself part of humanity.

But all the time he wanted to rise far above the earth. One night the idea of centrifugal force as the answer came to him. Feverishly, he plunged into work in his dank room, and soon there was a box on his workbench—a closed box, inside of which two pendulums vibrated, with balls fastened to their upper ends. He beamed at the circular arcs made by the balls as they moved. He was sure that their centrifugal force would carry the box into "Cosmos"—to the never-ending expanses of interplanetary space.

The night he finished building the box and saw the balls moving, he could not sleep. "I just wandered in the streets of Moscow and thought about the great consequences of my invention. But by morning I understood its futility, and the disillusionment was as sharp as the illusion had been." It would be years before he would return to the problems of space flight. He had yet much to learn.

So he went back to Feodor Petrushevsky's famous books on physics and Dmitry Mendeleyev's *Principles of Chemistry*. He posed himself problems, he solved them, he experimented. Acids left spots and holes in his trousers, and boys in the streets mocked him: "Have the mice eaten your pants?" He wore his hair long, for he lacked both the time and the money for barbering.

IV

Konstantin's father had moved his family to Vyatka, northeastern Russia, in the Urals. Money was scarcer than ever, and Eduard had already heard that his son in Moscow was starving himself into a walking skeleton. It was time for Konstantin to return.

In 1876, at nineteen, Konstantin left Moscow for Vyatka. Two years later the family moved back west to Ryazan, and Konstantin with them. He helped the brood's larder by private tutoring.

By then he had discovered in himself the enthusiasm and skill to talk to children, to tell them of nature's wonders and man's ability to transform nature. His father and others thought he would make a good schoolteacher. Konstantin heartily agreed.

In 1879, at twenty-two, still without going to any high school or college, he took an examination and passed it well. He now had his diploma as "a people's schoolteacher," the lowest rank in the czarist educational system, but of much satisfaction to Konstantin. Next year he was appointed to teach arithmetic, geometry, and physics at the Borovskoye district school in the Province of Kaluga, some forty-five miles southwest of Moscow.

Konstantin had a small flat of his own instead of just a room, and at once he turned this into a laboratory, where, in a description by a Russian biographer, "lightnings flashed, peals of thunder reverberated, bells rang and fires blazed, wheels revolved, and bright illuminations were switched on." When curious visitors came, Konstantin would blandly offer them some invisible jam. As they took spoons, electric shocks would astonish them. He built what he called an electric octopus, and this, in Tsiolkovsky's own later reminiscence, "caught the unwary visitor with its feelers by the nose or finger and then the victim's hair stood on end and sparks flew from his body."

In Borovsk, that little town surrounded by a pine forest and dotted with tanneries, miles away from the nearest railroad and certainly from the world of universities and scientists, he continued his solitary researches with the scantiest of books and equipment. In 1881, at twenty-four, he established and described the foundations of the kinetic theory of gases—not knowing that these had been discovered and published all of his twenty-four years before. He mailed off his paper to St. Petersburg to the Society of Physics and Chemistry, and its leaders gravely read and approved it while remarking that this young man had come upon these principles by his own sweat and thought. Among such approvers was Mendeleyev himself.

Encouraged, Tsiolkovsky chose the mechanics of a living organism as his second major theme. He sent his paper to the same society, and this time the reception was even better. The paper won a blessing from Professor Ivan Sechenov, the famous physiologist; and this led to Tsiolkovsky's acceptance as a member of the learned society, quite an honor to the young, self-tutored provincial.

But local people viewed Konstantin's labors with derision mixed with fear. As he walked through the little town's weed-grown streets, past its one-storied wooden houses and long gray fences, his thoughts were trillions of miles away. Engrossed, he would fail to notice the people he met and would not greet even his acquaintances and school superiors. Just as absentmindedly he left behind books, manuscripts, and also parts of machinery he was using in his experiments.

And yet occasionally he would be the very soul of that half-curious, half-hostile society of Borovsk. Once he built a large vulture with a wing span of about seventy centimeters. His construction was ingenious; his knowledge of air currents, superb. The vulture soared over the town, to the great merriment of adults no less than children.

In winter he skated on the local river with an umbrella in his adroit hands, adding velocity to his progress and one more spectacle to the town's amusements. He also fitted an armchair with sled runners, put a sail over it, and thus raced along the frozen stream, his windburned face ecstatic. "Peasants used to drive their sleds on that river, and horses reared while drivers cursed," Tsiolkovsky later reminisced. "But because I was deaf I didn't for a long time realize all the commotion I was causing."

Humanity outside the little town of Borovsk knew little or nothing of him. Except for the few leading members of the Society of Physics and Chemistry in St. Petersburg, no one in the world at large seemed either to hear or care about him; yet stubbornly the lone genius went on with his work. It was about this period of his life that Tsiolkovsky later said, "The chief goal of my life was not to waste my years but to help mankind in its progress even if a little. What interested me gave me neither bread nor influence but I hoped, and still hope, that my work will—perhaps soon, perhaps in the far-off future—give society mountains of bread and an incalculable amount of power."

Though himself lacking power and quite often even food, he cheerfully married Varvara Sokolova, a colleague's daughter. Used from childhood to pedagogical poverty, she made a wonderful wife. The marriage proved long and successful despite all the scarcities and privations.

In spite of the constant difficulties, he was hardly ever fainthearted and seldom depressed. At all times he dreamed and worked evenly, steadily, never in peaks and valleys.

V

At Borovsk, Tsiolkovsky once more tried to think and write about outer space. He had for a time forsaken his idea of centrifugal force and really had nothing scientific to offer in its stead. He thought he would study air, its ingredients, and its properties before he would suggest any modes of travel through it. And so, his very first published paper, an article printed in 1881, was "On the Resistance of Air."

Two years later he prepared a more ambitious work called "Free Space." In this he gave his analysis of the phenomena of physics that man might be able to observe were he able to penetrate interplanetary space. Here he also included his first diagram of an interplanetary ship to be moved by what we would now define as jet propulsion. But this work remained unpublished for some time.

"Free Space" had the form of a diary, but it was a systematic study of various problems of mechanics in a space entirely free of gravity and resistance. Weightlessness, so much a concern to us now, found an early prober in Tsiolkovsky.

He read hungrily all that he could find in his Borovsk isolation. Even in Russian classics of fiction he sought food for his scientific bent and thoughts. Of all of Ivan Turgenev's works, for instance, he singled out *Fathers and Sons*, most likely for its austere, fierce Yevgeni Bazarov and his fanatical belief in science and materialism.

Yet he did not share Bazarov's disdain for arts and beauty. In fact, Tsiolkovsky at times interlarded his theorizing, experimenting, and blueprinting with his exercises in science fiction. In 1887 he wrote a novelette entitled *On the Moon*; five years passed before a juvenile magazine published it. His other novelettes were *Daydreaming of Sky and Earth* and *Outside the Earth*. He also wrote fairy tales and poems about stars, about interplanetary travels, about mankind's future away from this earth.

Still, the greatest part of his time was devoted to more exact disciplines. Three large problems occupied Tsiolkovsky after 1884. The first one was the working-out of a scientific basis for an all-metal dirigible or aerostat. (For many years Russians used the dignified word "aerostat" for balloons as well as dirigibles.) The second concerned a streamlined airplane. The third had to do with a rocket for interplanetary travel. In all three, in all that thinking, diagraming, and tinkering, he was well ahead of his time—for Russia, if not for the West.

Tsiolkovsky's dirigible researches and theorizing were carried on from 1885 to 1892. It was in 1886 that he completed his first essay on the subject, "Theory and Experiment of an Aerostat." Therein he presented his scientific and technologic explanation of what a metal-surfaced dirigible could be. He supplied his speculative paper with blueprints containing all the chief details of such a dirigible. A summary of Tsiolkovsky's ideas of an all-metal dirigible was published many years later in 1905–1908 in a Russian aeronautical magazine under the title "The Aerostat and the Airplane." Yet later, in 1934, the Soviet editors of another collection of Tsiolkovsky's works declared that even at that time his early prevision of the dirigible was beyond any criticism and that no reliable scientist could "introduce any corrections to the formulas or conclusions given" by Tsiolkovsky in 1885 and repeated two decades later.

From 1934 to this day, Tsiolkovsky's Russian enthusiasts have said that, though, of course, not the world's very first proposal for a dirigible, his was a great improvement on its predecessors. If built as proposed, this would have been the first dirigible to have change-able capacity, the latter enabling the ship to have the same lifting power at variable temperatures of the surrounding air and in different altitudes of flight.

Soviet admirers of Tsiolkovsky say that, first, he would have controlled his airship's capacity with the aid of a special goffered (corrugated) cover of the dirigible as well as the help of "a shrinking system."

Secondly, Tsiolkovsky planned to warm up the gas filling the dirigible by the heat of the worked-off gases passing through coiled pipes. (Western critics of this plan now point out that thermodynamically this would have been impossible unless energy was added to the worked-off gas, but that Tsiolkovsky apparently made no provisions for any such supplemental power.)

Thirdly, Tsiolkovsky's goffered cover, although of thin metal, would have been treated for durability by the inventor's special devices; and its goffer pieces were placed by him, for the same purpose of durability, perpendicularly to the axis of the dirigible.

The geometrical shape of his dirigible and the exact, correct calculations of the durability of its thin metal cover were pioneered by Tsiolkovsky alone. So say Soviet rooters for Tsiolkovsky, and in at least some of these claims they may be right.

But the project was too bold for its sluggish era. Tsiolkovsky filed it now with one czarist office, now with another. Everywhere it was turned down. Even the general staff of the Russian army, in some respects so daring (it was among the first to make military use of Alexander Graham Bell's telephone and of British-made underwater torpedoes in the Russo-Turkish War of 1877–1878), saw no practical features in Tsiolkovsky's gas-filled, metal-covered bird. He was refused even the comparatively few rubles he needed to build its first model.

VI

And yet, not all was ill fortune for him. Two Russian scientists interested in problems of flying had heard of Tsiolkovsky's ideas. They were Nikolai Zhukovsky, now called by the Soviets "father of Russian aviation" (Moscow's foremost air academy is named after him), and Alexander Stoletov. An invitation from them brought young Tsiolkovsky to Moscow in the summer of 1887. The two scientists arranged for Konstantin to speak of his "aerostat" at a meeting of the Physics Division of the Moscow Society of Nature Knowledge Lovers. Tsiolkovsky's paper was heard with considerable appreciation.

In 1892 he transferred some of his ideas and diagrams to the printed page of his book *The Aerostat, Metallic and Directed.* A few readers sent in their praise, but there was no governmental acclaim nor a subsidy from anyone for going ahead and building the machine.

Still there was a slight improvement in his affairs. In 1892 Tsiolkovsky moved from his county town to Kaluga, the provincial capital ninety miles southwest of Moscow, and to a somewhat better position: he became a high school teacher. He was destined to teach in Kaluga for some forty years.

At first, besides his main job as instructor of physics and mathematics in a girls' parochial school, he was given a similar assignment in a boys' ghimnaziya, the classical high school. But one being a religious school and the other placing an emphasis on Latin and Greek, neither stressed his beloved disciplines. Possibly, it was just as well. He was left with more time and thought for his own researches and inventions.

In Kaluga, in his mid-thirties, Tsiolkovsky continued his work in the new and little-known field of heavier-than-air flying ships. He came forth with an idea for an airplane built around a metal frame. In 1894 the magazine *Nauka i zhizn'* ("Science and Life") published his article "Airplane, or Birdlike (Aviational) Flying Machine." Therein he blueprinted and described a monoplane, and this included his minute calculations of the plane's physics and mathematics. His Russian biographers now insist that, by its exterior appearance and its aerodynamic components, his monoplane of 1894 was certainly a prevision of airplanes that first actually appeared fifteen and eighteen years later. The biographers praise its wings with their "thick profile," its rounded leading edge, and its streamlined fuselage.

As earlier in Borovsk, so for many new years in Kaluga people laughed at him: "He thinks an iron balloon can fly in the air! Here is a crank for you!" "A dreamer," "a utopian," were the mildest epithets.

Yet, gradually, a few—very few—admirers or at least congenial spirits appeared too. Some lived in Kaluga; others, not so near, but they wrote to Tsiolkovsky often. In Kaluga itself the Assonov family and also a druggist of vague English origin named P. P. Cunning came forth with their warmth and even a few rubles to help Tsiolkovsky. There was a faithful correspondent from the Upper Volga region—Sergei Shcherbakov, president of the Nizhny Novgorod Circle of Lovers of Physics and Astronomy. In 1895 Shcherbakov began the publication of Russia's first annual astronomic calendar. Later he moved to Kaluga.

Tsiolkovsky felt heartened as he went on to his new and yet newer experiments. In 1897 he built an "aerodynamic pipe"—a wind tunnel, the first in Russia. He suggested methods of wind-tunnel experiments and, in 1900, finally securing a money grant from the Academy of Sciences (quite possibly with Mendeleyev's help), carried out the "blowing" or "scavenging" of some simple models; he also ascertained coefficients of resistance of spheres, flat plates, cylinders, cones, and other bodies.

The Academy's grant of 470 rubles (in American money equal to about $235) was a small sum, but a marvelous moral victory. This, however, was not followed by any other such recognitions of Tsiolkovsky's genius by men powerful in Russia's science of the time.

In 1904 a prominent Moscow newspaper with a national circulation publicized some of Tsiolkovsky's ideas and strivings and said the man deserved at least some public support. The newspaper announced that it would accept donations for Tsiolkovsky. By 1906 some five hundred rubles were collected, and Tsiolkovsky asked for the money. No, said the editors, let us wait a while longer for more contributions. Three more years passed, fruitlessly, and in 1909 the five hundred rubles were finally handed to the scientist.

In its long career, his small, lean Kaluga laboratory burned completely on one occasion and was flooded on another. He had to rebuild and restock it by denying himself and his family some more of their necessities. His parochial schoolgirls noticed the awful state of his winter clothes and footwear; they took up a collection among themselves and bought their teacher a pair of rubbers. He accepted the gift in silence, but the girls saw two tears slowly coursing down his sunken cheeks and straggly beard.

At times the schoolgirls walked with him after the lessons in the direction of his house. He talked to them of wonderful interstellar journeys of the future. "He would say goodbye to us beyond a bridge where, in impassable mud, lay the street at the end of which his house stood," a former pupil recalled in the 1950s. "Rain poured, dusk thickened, but we were reluctant to start back for our homes. For this meant no more of that afternoon's inspired, miraculous monologue about mankind's future."

In class, while listening through his antiquated tin horn to a pupil's recitation, he would sometimes jump up from his chair, shouting, "I've found it! I've found it!" He would rush to his notebooks on the desk, feverishly write down his discoveries, then, beaming, turn back to the class.

But still his mind was only half with his pupils.

He wanted to press on with his wind-tunnel ideas, his dirigible plan, and so many other of his fertile schemes. But he was stopped again and again by the many hours he had to give to teaching and by the lack of materials, of assistants, above all of money.

Rockets, increasingly, were Tsiolkovsky's chief absorption. He thought and dreamed of rockets incessantly. He saw man—he saw himself—go up, up, into the universe. Some thirty years after that night in Moscow when, as a youth in his late teens, he had paced the streets thinking he had discovered a way of floating into the cosmos, the old vision of flying to the stars would come back to haunt him delectably. "Now, these thirty years later," he confessed, "I still dream at night that in my machine I am rising to the stars, and I experience the same exaltation I did that long-ago night in Moscow."

VII

Already in 1883, at the age of twenty-six, Tsiolkovsky wrote that "reactive movement"—jet and rocket propulsion in our era's language—should be considered as a force for flying. Toward the end of the 1890s he began to evolve a mathematical theory of such propulsion.

From 1896 on, Tsiolkovsky was spending much of his time on the idea of "the reactive apparatus." It was beginning with this period that he gave himself over increasingly to rocketry, constantly blue-printing and at every chance publishing his schemes of "rockets of long-distance action"—most specifically, rockets for interplanetary journeys.

When, within the next fifteen years, he completed this phase of his theorizing, the result in the estimate of his modern Soviet devotees was a solution of utmost magnitude. According to one recent Soviet biographer, Professor Arkady A. Kosmodemiansky (himself a doctor of the physical and mathematical sciences and a rocket specialist on motion of bodies with variable mass), "Tsiolkovsky discovered and studied in detail the equation of the rocket motion with constant exhaust velocity and arrived at a very important mathematical result known as 'the Tsiolkovsky Formula.'"

Here, notably, Soviet Russians and at least some Western scientists still differ on the value of Tsiolkovsky's contribution. Some Western doubters call his theory and formula mostly a hodgepodge of generalities, interspersed with some originality and fact. They question Tsiolkovsky's priority in whatever they do find valuable in his writing about rockets.

But in their praise of "the Tsiolkovsky Formula," his Russian admirers point out that much of this solution can already be found in his first significant paper on the subject of rockets, "Exploitation of Cosmic Expanse Via Reactive Equipment" (in some English-language references also called "Investigating Space with Reaction Devices"). Finishing this paper in January 1903, Tsiolkovsky sent it to the St. Petersburg magazine *Nauchnoye obozreniye* ("Scientific Review"). The editor was impressed and accepted it at once; yet as his second thought in publishing the article, he put in his apologetic editorial addendum that "the author's fantasy flew too far off."

The article was so long that it had to be run in two installments.

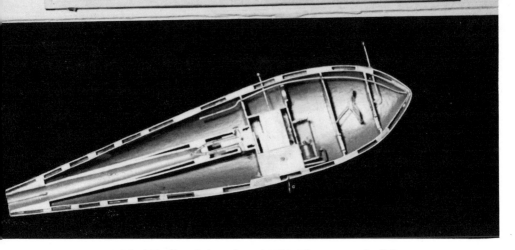

A model of Tsiolkovsky's rocket of 1903. The sign reads: "The impossible of today will become possible tomorrow." *Sovfoto*

The first part appeared in the May 1903 issue of the magazine, but the magazine, although scientific, was suspect for its political overtones. Such Marxists as Vladimir Lenin and George Plekhanov were among its contributors. The czar's gendarmes closed the magazine and seized all its papers, including manuscripts accepted but not yet published. The magazine never came out again.

Tsiolkovsky either had a copy of the second part of his article or succeeded in having the unpublished installment returned to him. But it was only eight years later, in 1911, that with the aid of his friends and followers he finally published the second and final part in the St. Petersburg magazine *Viestnik vozdukhoplavaniya* ("Herald of Aeronautics").

Most likely, he did not leave the text of the second part in its original form, but added to it whatever he had learned or calculated in the intervening years. He went on to expound his theory of a rocket's flight involving the changes of the rocket's mass in the process of its movement. It was in this paper as a whole that he first discussed the possible use of rockets to investigate upper strata of the atmosphere and, at some future time, for interplanetary communication. It was here that he advanced the idea of building and launching satellites to orbit around the earth.

But in Russia on the eve of the First World War, officials paid little attention to his work. True, in November 1914, a few months after the war's outbreak, one of Tsiolkovsky's projects reached the bureaucratic heights of the Chief Artillery Office. At a session of generals and professors of artillery, his blueprints were studied— and declined. A Russian émigré now living in the United States recalls that as a young aide he was present at that conference: "Tsiolkovsky's name was completely unknown to those at the conference. The rocket he proposed was meant by him not for artillery but for interplanetary flights, a subject entirely strange to the era's artillery men."

In one of his brochures published in 1914, Tsiolkovsky himself wrote bitterly: "How difficult it is to work for years all alone under unfavorable circumstances and not to see any light or help from anywhere."

Fifteen years later, in 1929, Tsiolkovsky came out with two detailed proposals of multistage rockets. It may be argued that in America Dr. Goddard had already worked out and made public this multistage principle in 1914; but Tsiolkovsky's Soviet fans stubbornly persist in their conviction that the Kaluga wizard antedated the Worcester professor at least with hints of this principle scattered in the Russian's earlier writings and that in 1929 Tsiolkovsky merely spelled out in detail what he had, years earlier, brainstormed in general.

The first of Tsiolkovsky's two proposals of 1929 is familiar to us all today: it is the firing of rockets attached to one another, in a sequence, beginning with the lowest, each with an increasing velocity, until the head rocket is the only one left; and this is all that reaches its destination (the principle used in the sputniks and in our own satellites). Tsiolkovsky called this tandem string "a rocket train."

The second type suggested by Tsiolkovsky is a parallel instead of a tandem connection of several rockets. Tsiolkovsky called it *eskadrillia* or "a flying squadron." Here all the interconnected rockets are fired and work simultaneously, until one-half of their fuel is expended. Then the outer engines pour their remaining fuel into the half-empty tanks of the other rockets and fall off. The remaining rockets continue on their upward way at an increasing speed. The process is repeated until just one rocket remains—the head one. This last rocket develops an enormous speed en route to its final destination.

Tsiolkovsky knew his fuel propellants. For rockets he recommended combinations of liquid hydrogen and liquid oxygen, of alcohol and liquid oxygen, of hydrocarbons and liquid oxygen or ozone, of kerosene and liquid oxygen, and of methane and liquid oxygen.

Today's Russians claim for Tsiolkovsky the solution of the question of fuel needed for a rocket to overcome the earth's gravity and atmosphere. He also thought of fuels as coolants. He knew that the walls of the combustion chamber of a jet-propelled ship must be cooled and wrote that such cooling could be done by components of fuel. The Russians now comment that this method of cooling, as used in modern jets and rockets, stems from Tsiolkovsky's suggestion and no one else's. Western experts argue that Goddard and another American, James H. Wyld, and also the Austrian scientist-engineer Count Guido von Pirquet had been first here too. It is extremely difficult to sort out laurels in this particular area; yet it may be said with some certainty that at least Wyld cannot qualify for priority in rocket coolants: his use of fuel as a coolant of the rocket's combustion chamber was demonstrated as late as December 1938.

Possibly at the same time as this idea was tried out in the West, possibly earlier, Tsiolkovsky suggested that liquid oxidizers could effectively be employed to cool the rocket's exteriors. He investigated a number of oxidizers, appraising them for this role.

Doubtless, he was among the first to write about sending up interplanetary platforms as in-between stations en route to the moon, Mars, and other celestial bodies. He discoursed in detail on the possible conditions under which man could live on artificial satellites and interplanetary platforms.

Tsiolkovsky also advanced the idea of "gas-powered" steering equipment for rockets navigating in the airless expanse. He suggested gyroscopic stabilization of the rocket in its free flight through space, where there is neither gravity nor any force of resistance.

VIII

The problem of rockets' reentry was among Tsiolkovsky's early preoccupations. He worked out special trajectories for rockets to decelerate their speed on their reentry of the atmosphere and so safeguard them against excessive friction and consequent disintegration.

When in 1954 the Soviet Academy of Sciences published volume 2 of Tsiolkovsky's collected works, even a partial list of its contents and their respective dates showed how deservedly he was already then called a pioneer of rocket dynamics and of the theory of space flight. The volume included, among others:

"Free Space," 1883
"Investigating Space with Reaction Devices," 1903 and 1911; revised in 1914 and 1926.
"The Spaceship," 1924.
"The Space Rocket, an Essay," 1927.
"The New Airplane," 1927.
"Cosmic Step Rockets," 1929.
"The Jet Airplane," 1930.
"To Astronauts," 1930.
"Ascending Acceleration of the Rocket-Plane," 1930.
"The Semi-Jet Stratoplane," 1932.
"Reaching the Stratosphere, Rocket Fuel," 1934.
"The Maximum Speed of a Rocket," 1935.

In 1911, Tsiolkovsky wrote that "only a searching mind and science could show the way" toward changing the phenomena of rocket propulsion "into something vast, almost beyond the range of our perception." That year, with utter conviction, he wrote of a new, great era that would start from the very first moment of man's use of jet propulsion and rockets. Man would be able "to step on the soil of asteroids; to pick up a stone from the moon with his own hand; to organize interplanetary platforms; to form rings—with life on them—around the earth, the moon, and the sun; to observe Mars at close quarters; to land on the satellites of Mars or even on Mars itself."

The Soviets now stoutly maintain that Tsiolkovsky's work of 1903–1911 alone establishes his trailblazing in the most modern applications of rocketry, particularly as concerns the multistage principle. They declare that the very first mathematical proof of the rocket's use in solving scientific problems was his, and his alone. They do not admit that any Western scientist might have proposed or solved any such applications simultaneously, unknowingly, or at least just as fully and brilliantly. They insist that the idea of using rockets in the construction of huge interplanetary ships is entirely Tsiolkovsky's and no one else's. He was the world's very first scien-

tist, they say, to present the basic theory of the liquid-propelled jet
engine, along with the theory of the elements of that engine's
construction.

They attach the name of "the Tsiolkovsky Formula" to almost all
early analysis of the connection between the speed acquired by a
rocket, the rate of the flow of gases from the rocket's engine, the
rocket's entire weight, and the weight of the fuel carried by the
rocket. They give him practically all the credit for man's first defini-
tion of this fundamental interrelation in rocketry.

In 1911, Tsiolkovsky, according to the Soviets, was among the
first, if not indeed the very first, to point to nuclear processes, also
to electronic and ionic engines, as a source of energy for future
rockets.

Even the shape of today's rocket harks back to Tsiolkovsky's early
designs—just look at them in our museums, Moscow invites urgent-
ly. But, above all, by being the very first to suggest artificial satellites for the earth and for presaging their scientific principles so
astonishingly, Tsiolkovsky is certainly the original father of all the
Sputnik, Lunik, Explorer, Vanguard, Vostok, Saturn-Apollo, and
other achievements. So say the Soviets.

What is the truth? Where are the Soviets right in these claims
and where are they wrong? For every comparative chronology of
Russian and Western "firsts" in rocketry, worked out by the Soviets
to their glory, the West can surely produce a similarly disputatious
and impressive chart to its advantage. For each Western insistence
on an invention or discovery, there could be—has been—a counter-
pretense, particularly by the Soviets. Even where a major priority is
clearly established for one country, another nation can show that
certain necessary preliminaries to the invention in question were
discovered within its borders.

Still, this much has been said in the West of Tsiolkovsky for
certain. The late Willy Ley, the celebrated German-American rocket expert, from his own early and authentic experience testified that
in one of the most important features of rocket propulsion—propellants—Tsiolkovsky anticipated the Germans, particularly Oberth,
by twenty years, and that the Russian was ahead of America's
own Dr. Goddard by some fourteen years. Ley stated, "Tsiolkovsky, Goddard, and Oberth—in that chronological order

—predicted that high-performance rockets would result from the utilization of liquid fuels."

In another connection, dwelling on the early German efforts to control the direction of a rocket's motion and also on the discovery that "control surfaces should act against the exhaust stream rather than against the air stream," Ley recognized that "Tsiolkovsky had thought of that first."

Why did not Tsiolkovsky take out rocket patents ahead of Goddard or Oberth and other Westerners? Ley's valid explanation was that Tsiolkovsky mostly mused and blueprinted instead of actually experimenting as Goddard and the Germans did. Indeed, Tsiolkovsky dreamed and diagramed the use of liquids in rocket propulsion long before all others did, but his trouble lay precisely in the fact that he was too well in front.

Dr. Walter R. Dornberger, who in World War II was Germany's general in charge of the Nazi rocket center at Peenemunde, said to this writer after the war when Dornberger worked for an American rocket plant, "Tsiolkovsky was the earliest pioneer of all and suffered because he was so early." Tsiolkovsky (Dornberger explained) was penalized and handicapped the worst by his era's three acute lacks: "No light metals were then available for good rocket construction. Liquid oxygen as a propellant was yet unknown. And, of course, there was no reliable electronic equipment."

All three ingredients began to appear practically years after Tsiolkovsky had been the first to speak up theoretically. All three were used by Americans and Germans before the Russians managed to get around to the practical phase. Goddard and Oberth, among others, showed this pragmatic readiness to apply, in addition to their ability to speculate and analyze.

When Oberth's first major book was published in 1923, Tsiolkovsky complained to a friend that he, Tsiolkovsky, had published the very same ideas before: ". . . space helmets, multistage rockets . . . a black sky, nontwinkling stars . . . manned space platforms as way stations to further space travel, orbiting around the earth, even the 200-ton weight of the rocket to lift the astronauts."

But it was only in 1925, two years after Oberth's volume was published, that its author first heard of Tsiolkovsky. In 1929, the

German nobly wrote to Tsiolkovsky: "Of course I would be the last to dispute your priority and your merits in the field of rockets. My only regret is that I had not heard of you before 1925. Had I known your excellent work, I would have surely been further along in my own research—I would have spared myself much unnecessary labor." And again: "You lighted the light, and we will work until mankind's dream comes true."

IX

The Soviets now insist that only their government could and did give Tsiolkovsky all the recognition and aid he had so long merited, but failed to receive. This was not true of the early phase of the Soviet regime, however. It is a fact that in 1919 Tsiolkovsky was elected to the Socialist Academy (founded in June 1918, renamed Communist Academy in 1924, merged with the regular Academy of Sciences in 1936), but of material aid there was at first very little. Returning from his visit to Russia in 1920, H. G. Wells wrote that as the result of the war collapse and the revolutionary chaos of the time, the Russian "scientific worker found himself with a salary of rubles that dwindled rapidly to less than the five-hundredth part of their original value." He was shocked to meet world-renowned Russian scientists as ragged, hungry men, devoid of any sense of being wanted. Wells explained this low state of scientists and other men of culture:

> The new crude social organization, fighting robbery, murder, and the wildest disorder, had no place for them; it had forgotten them. For the scientific man at first the Soviet government had as little regard as the first French Revolution, which had "no need for chemists."

Conditions improved slowly, and the new Soviet concern for the scientist was felt in large cities sooner than in Kaluga. In time it reached Tsiolkovsky too.

He was given first a regular subsidy; later, a pension—both small, but enough to survive on and to continue his work. His books and articles were now being printed at public expense. Between 1917 and 1935 three times as many of his books, brochures, and articles were published as had seen the printed page in all the long decades of his life and struggle before the revolution; the score was 150 and 50 titles respectively. In the seven-year period of 1925–1932 alone, some 60 of his works on physics, astronomy, mechanics, and philosophy appeared. He was being interviewed and photographed. He was even briefly filmed for the cinema. His mail grew voluminously; and, however late, even foreign scientists now wrote to him, some rather admiringly. One devotee of Tsiolkovsky perhaps more than any other was responsible for this discovery of the Kaluga hermit. He was a Leningrad science writer and editor, Dr. Yakov I. Perelman. It was his untiring trumpeting of Tsiolkovsky's visions that made the man famous as well as comfortable, even if so late in life.

Tsiolkovsky at last felt free to do many things he had skipped or skimped on earlier in his career. At the sunset of his days, he intermittently turned from his beloved rockets to that early interest of his—the dirigible. In October 1932, he wrote to a friend, "The field of dirigibles has opportunities that cannot even be imagined." Two months later he was involved in a project to build "a large transatlantic hydroplane, seating thirty to one hundred persons and able to cruise within a range of five to ten thousand kilometers."

He wrote not only on aerodynamics, but also on the future sociopolitical structure of human colonies to be established on those artificial islands of the future, whirling around the sun somewhere between the orbits of the earth and Mars. He wrote about Soviet industries and the ways of improving their technology.

Tsiolkovsky ventured into such disciplines as philosophy and linguistics, but here—as indeed in some of his aerodynamic theories and projects—not all was accepted as valid even by his Soviet admirers. At times he himself was not too sure of his supreme wisdom. Thirteen months before his death, he wrote to a Russian engineer:

> My ideas on the universe seem to me the only scientific ideas possible. It is, of course, subjective of me to say so. Let us grant that I am a sage. But in other times there were many sages. And all of them made mistakes—did not possess the entire truth. This is the very thing I think about myself as I think of that historical verity. One thing I am sure of: My ideas are not harmful for either believers or disbelievers.

As "disbelievers" he classed "persons of pure science." These, he said, could not believe in God. The former teacher of the parochial school was now, by his life's close, an atheist; but there is no evidence that he ever became a member of the Communist party.

X

In 1932, at the age of seventy-five, he was yet vigorous enough to ride a bicycle as his customary means of getting around Kaluga. That year he accepted as his due the pompous celebrations arranged for him by the Soviet government in honor of his reaching the three-quarters-of-a-century milestone.

In 1933, the very first Soviet-built rocket was at last sent up from a Moscow airdrome to a height of a few miles. On hearing the news, Tsiolkovsky tore around a room in great excitement. A young engineer tried to calm him: "But, Konstantin Eduardovich, the rocket rose to such an insignificant height."

Tsiolkovsky wheeled at the man in anger and eloquence. "Remember the first flight in an airplane!" he cried. "Not many understood then that a new era was dawning. The same is true of this first rocket launching. It opens a new page in man's conquest of endless expanses—with the aid of rockets. The hour is not far off when Soviet rocket ships will rush off into great airless expanses. And this will happen in our twentieth century!"

He had been that optimistic most of his working years. He looked at life with a morning freshness even when, at last, he found himself at the hurricane's eye of a major change in human history. But his years were finally drawing to their end—before he would see the glory of the true rocket age. He was ailing; he was growing feeble.

In 1935, during the May Day demonstration, he spoke to the marchers in Moscow's Red Square over the radio; and in his speech he conjured up a vision of flocks of interstellar ships rising from Soviet fields in some not-too-distant future. The phonograph record of that talk is often played in Russia these days.

As the Soviet government thanked him with the Order of the Red Banner of Labor, he felt impelled to thank the government: "Only our Soviet government has treated me humanely. The new and real motherland has provided conditions fit for life and work. I am proud of my country, yes, proud."

And he urged the youth of the Soviet Union: "Komsomol

members and young men and women, study hard. Study with a light heart. Do not for a moment forget about the future of our great country!"

Some of Tsiolkovsky's young Russian friends during World War II found themselves in the West and refused to return home. One of them, now in the United States, tells us that toward the end of Tsiolkovsky's life the Soviet government, while encouraging his rocket work, forbade the publication of his philosophic writings.

According to this source, Tsiolkovsky in 1934–1935 was uneasy. He knew he was dying of cancer. He worried about his family. On what income were they to exist after he was gone? Six days before his death, he wrote a letter to the Central Committee of the Communist Party, bequeathing all his works on aviation, rocketry, and interplanetary travel "to the Bolshevik party and the Soviet government." In this way, his friends abroad now say, he was trying to win a posthumous pension for his family.

Two days later, on Tsiolkovsky's seventy-eighth birthday, Stalin replied with a telegram thanking him for his letter and wishing him good health. In two more days, on September 19, 1935, Tsiolkovsky was dead.

His library, manuscripts, models, and other memorabilia were at first taken to the central offices of Aeroflot, but later put into a museum or two. Tsiolkovsky's old house in Kaluga is now such a museum, some of his books and things having apparently been returned to the old place. The Nazis, occupying Kaluga during the war, destroyed or carried off some of the exhibits. Most of the latter were, however, saved by the staff of the museum or otherwise restored. Tsiolkovsky's old one-story house is now one of the nation's shrines, a mecca for school children, army detachments, and tourists from all over the country and lately from abroad too, particularly from East European countries.

In 1952 the Aeroclub of France minted a large gold medal in honor of Tsiolkovsky. In 1954 the Soviet government established the Tsiolkovsky Gold Medal to be awarded every three years for the most outstanding contribution to the advancement of interplanetary navigation. In 1957 the Leningrad Studio of Scientific-Popular Films made a full-length motion picture *The Road to the Stars*, devoted to the life and toil of Tsiolkovsky. Old newsreels of the

1930s showing Tsiolkovsky at work and rest were interlarded with the reenaction of his inspired fervors by one of Russia's best actors. Much of the film was made on location in Kaluga.

In the late spring of 1958 a monument to Tsiolkovsky was unveiled in Kaluga. A silvery upright model of a rocket, nineteen meters high, is the background for Tsiolkovsky's bronze figure. The granite pedestal bears the inscription K. E. TSIOLKOVSKY, 1857–1935, and this prophecy from his writings of 1913: "Mankind will not remain on earth forever, but in its quest of light and space will at first timidly penetrate beyond the confines of the atmosphere and later will conquer for itself all the space near the sun."

7. PETER KAPITSA
Faithful Sentinel of Non-Marxist Science

IF you ask any scientist anywhere, East or West, for the name of the Soviet scientist best known to him, the chances are overwhelming that you will receive the answer, "Peter Kapitsa, of course." The name is indeed well known the world over, but not the man himself. Despite the many years of his appearance in the world's headlines, Academician Peter (Pyotr) Leonidovich Kapitsa is something of a mystery, and not only to other nations, but to his fellow Russians as well.

One of the earliest Russians to come back to the Soviet Union from a prolonged experience abroad and surely one of the most important among such repatriates, Kapitsa has never publicly explained certain intriguing details about his return in 1934 and has never revealed the complete historical facts of what happened between him and Stalin. As C. P. Snow has written, "Among the conversations which I should most like to have listened to, I put high those between Kapitsa and Stalin." So far, for reasons personal or political, Dr. Kapitsa has refrained from putting those conversa-

Peter Kapitsa in 1938. *Soviet Life from Sovfoto*

tions—or any other details of his detention by Stalin—on record. Because such details are still not quite clear, they have to be reported in this work by hearsay and almost on speculation.

The extent of Kapitsa's reconciliation with the Communist regime, which practically kidnapped him, is an enigma. To some observers, equally debatable is the degree to which he may be viewed as a center or a symbol of the present-day active opposition of one group within the New Class against another, of scientists against political bosses.

Some say that the great Russian physicist is a loyal Soviet patriot, even if not a member of the Communist party. At least one of the Russian defectors with whom I have talked expressed his doubt that Peter Kapitsa can be properly regarded as a source of opposition to the party. This man, a former industrial manager from Leningrad, remarked to me that Dr. Kapitsa "has been vastly overrated as harboring any true sense" of any such opposition and that "there is no real independence in him."

But I have found this a minority opinion. Others in speaking about Kapitsa recall the strange story of his detention by Josef Stalin, cite instances of his defiance of Stalin and his later differences with Nikita Khrushchev, and insist that he is still a rebel—a kind of "Peck's Bad Boy" of the Soviets.

In the last few years, Kapitsa has publicly denounced Communist dogmatists for their Stalin-begotten hostility to Einstein's theory of relativity, to electronic computers, to cybernetics as a whole. He has criticized Khrushchevian and post-Khrushchevian interference by Communist politicians in the daily affairs and long-range plans of Soviet science. His signature has been prominent among those daring Soviet scientists, writers, and other intellectuals who addressed to the Communist leaders formal and frank protests against the latest arrests that mark today's Kremlin policy. He has made no secret of liking the officially tabooed work of Soviet abstractionist artists and sculptors. In sum, the available evidence points to the fact that in his long but not too voluntary Soviet period, Peter Kapitsa has at times gone against the power that has tried to order him around. If not always in opposition, and certainly not the chief leader of any hidden or open "scientists' movement" against the Kremlin, Peter Kapitsa by his life and work does prove that the New Class is divided.

II

There are plenty of reasons why both Communists and non-Communists should admire Professor Kapitsa. Director of the Academy's far-famed Institute of Problems of Physics, he is one of Russia's foremost physicists, author of the hydrodynamic theory of bearing lubrication, originator of the hypothesis of spherical lightning, researcher and designer of equipment in heat transfer and super-fluidity of helium, and leading experimenter in atomic physics. His scholarly publications are numerous and important, and his work has earned for him a great number of Soviet and international honors and prizes.

Peter Leonidovich Kapitsa, born on July 8, 1894, comes of West Russian stock—from Belorussia, or White Russia. Peter's father, Leonid, was a lieutenant general in the Czar's Corps of Engineers; he helped to modernize the old naval base and fortress of Kronstadt, near St. Petersburg. Peter's mother, Olga, was a well-known teacher and collector of Russian folklore. Peter himself was born at Kronstadt. Some of the best schools of czarist Russia gave him his early education.

The Revolution of 1917 found Peter an honor student in the capital's Polytechnic Institute. His first scientific paper was published in the journal of the Russian Society of Physics and Chemistry the very month the Bolsheviks overthrew the liberal provisional government and proclaimed their Soviet republic. One of Kapitsa's official Communist biographers was, in time, to comment: "Life presents most incredible coincidences. Along with the new state a new scientist was born."

Graduating in 1918, the young man worked with Professor Abram F. Ioffe in the Physics-Technical Institute. Ioffe was Russia's earliest atomic physicist. By his side Kapitsa learned as much about the elusive atom as was known at the time. He also worked with Professor Nikolai Semyonov, who many years later (in 1956) won a Nobel Prize. In 1918–1920, Semyonov and Kapitsa collaborated in the development of an original method of ascertaining magnetic properties of the atom.

But Russia's civil war and its aftermath were not exactly conducive to the scientists' well-being and peace of mind. Amid the bloodshed and chaos of 1919–1921, the Kremlin had little thought for Russian savants. Plans of government-sponsored research remained on paper. For many scholars and their families there was neither food nor fuel. Some died amid privations. Several reports insist that among such victims were Kapitsa's wife and two babies and that Peter himself survived almost in spite of his will. Crushed, brooding, he decided to leave his homeland.

Soviet officials, at first, would not hear of a foreign journey for Kapitsa. Now that the civil war was over, the Soviet republic needed scientists for its reconstruction, they said. But Maxim Gorky, Russia's most influential writer then living, came to Kapitsa's rescue. In 1921, thanks to Gorky's intercession, as well as Ioffe's recommendation, a visa was granted to Kapitsa.

The official fiction was that the Academy of Sciences was sending him abroad as a member of a professorial delegation to renew contacts with foreign scholars and also to purchase sorely needed books and laboratory equipment. Shabbily dressed, thin, thoughtful, he sailed for London.

III

Later, Kapitsa would say that at the time no one in England knew him. But Ioffe was known, and he was along on this trip. He recommended Kapitsa as a young man of promise—a brilliant blend of powerful analyst and practical engineer. Ernest Rutherford at once made a place for Peter in his famous Cavendish Laboratory at Cambridge.

Lord Rutherford was the genius who discovered the nucleus of the atom and was the first to change the structure of an atom, but other problems of physics were also being researched at his laboratory. Kapitsa was in time recognized as the Old Wizard's favorite staff member. Under Rutherford's guidance, although never working with him on any common project, Kapitsa busied himself with the investigation of the reaction of matter to the influence of magnetic fields. His spirits soon revived; he was now increasingly confident and even gay.

Yet a few scientists did not exactly like Kapitsa—for reasons both personal and political. Among these men were his fellow Russian émigrés. They were definitely (and some belligerently) anti-Soviet, but young Kapitsa seemed equivocal at best. To some acquaintances he explained himself as not an émigré but an emissary, that is, a scientist still on a Moscow mission of research and purchase of equipment and books, with a vaguely acknowledged obligation someday to return home to the Soviets.

Professor Stepan Timoshenko, an émigré already then making a great name for himself in American academic and engineering circles for his work in theoretical and applied mechanics, met Kapitsa at a scientific congress in Edinburgh in September 1921. Years later, he recalled that even in his first few months at Cambridge, young Kapitsa "felt no lack of any of his necessities," because "the Bolshevik government furnished him with money fairly generously." It was this money, Timoshenko went on, that indirectly helped Kapitsa gain initial fame of a sort in England.

> He could even afford to buy a motorcycle. On this he began experimenting. He wanted to ascertain the utmost speed that could be attained on it. These experiments ended for him badly. On one occasion, while making a turn at high speed, the motorcycle crashed, and Kapitsa found himself in a ditch. The impact was considerable, but his arms and legs survived intact. His face and chest, however, did suffer. Someone picked Kapitsa up and delivered him to a hospital, where he had to remain for more than a week.

Telling of this adventure the very first evening of his meeting with Timoshenko at Edinburgh, Kapitsa related that in the hospital he "was bored waiting for a full recovery and so, his head still bandaged, went back to the laboratory." The effect was dramatic. One after another, his associates came to Kapitsa's cubicle, asked questions in awe, and wished him to get well soon. "Finally Rutherford himself made his appearance, gazed at the bandaged head, and left silently. This made Kapitsa rather well known in the laboratory."

Grudgingly, Timoshenko admitted that at the scientific congress in Edinburgh, at the university's dormitory where the visiting scientists were housed, the young and exuberant Kapitsa quickly proved himself to be as popular as apparently he had become at Cambridge.

> In the evening, when all gathered in the drawing room, he amused the public by his tricks and experiments. He was extraordinarily bold. When, in the course of an experiment, he needed an assistant, he would

unceremoniously pull some celebrated scientist by his sleeve and begin to explain to him just what it was he had to do. Solemn, dignified Englishmen lost their gravity of manner and fully submitted to Kapitsa's decisive actions.

IV

Some of Kapitsa's audacity may have come from his inner conviction that he had something of value to offer to these British and their society. Indeed, he did. As even Timoshenko allowed, "his superiority over young English scientists came from his passage through the excellent engineering school of the St. Petersburg Polytechnic Institute." He therefore could and did design large machinery. "In his scientific work he tended to shift from small physics equipment to big machines, and this change of the experiment's scale gave him a chance to carry out a series of important researches."

In 1923, Peter Kapitsa defended his dissertation and was awarded his doctorate by Cambridge. The same year brought him the James Clark Maxwell Prize, one of the world's highest scientific honors. In 1924 he developed unique equipment for work with superpowerful magnetic fields. More and more, the eyes of Britain's scientists were upon him. In 1929, Kapitsa was elected to the Royal Society, the first foreigner (so it was said) to receive this honor in two centuries. By the early 1930s he had been elected also to the British Institute of Physics, to the Cambridge Philosophical Society, and to Trinity College. He was presently a full professor at Cambridge. The Royal Society built a special laboratory to suit his exacting specifications. In 1932 he designed a high-production hydrogen liquefier. In 1934 he began blueprints of his original apparatus for producing large quantities of liquid oxygen (further developed and constructed in 1938). His administrative posts included an assistant directorship in the Cavendish Magnetic Research Laboratory and, from 1930, a directorship in the Cambridge University Laboratory.

The mutual respect between Rutherford and Kapitsa grew into a close friendship. Already in 1923 the British master considered the young Russian an outstanding star of the Cavendish Laboratory, "one of the finest scientific brains which even that great nursery of talent had ever seen." Early in 1925, Rutherford wrote in a letter to R. W. Boyle about Kapitsa's "big experiment for producing mag-netic fields" and gave enthusiastic details:

This research is being financed by the Government, and involves the installation in one of the old Engineering Laboratories of a complete power station with a 1500 kilowatt machine as the source of the power. It is a very elaborate experiment and I hope it will come off all right. If so, there will of course be a great deal of work to do in the examining of magnetic properties in these very high fields. The whole scheme will cost a good deal and will be financed by the Department of Scientific Research.

On December 17, 1925, Kapitsa wrote from the Cavendish Laboratory to Rutherford, then traveling for pleasure:

I am writing you this letter to Cairo to tell you that we already have the short circuit machine and the coil, and we managed to obtain fields over 270,000 [units] in a cylindrical volume of a diameter of 1 cm, and 4-1/2 cms high. We could not go further as the coil bursted with a great bang, which, no doubt, would amuse you very much, if you could hear it. . . .

At present all these experiments have been done with a higher speed machine, and I am very happy that everything went well, and now you may be quite sure 98 percent of the money is not wasted, and everything is working.

The accident was the most interesting of all the experiments, and gives the final touch of certainty, as we now know exactly what has happened when the coil bursted. . . . I am very impatient to see you again in the laboratory and to tell you all the little details, some of which are amusing, about the fight with the machines. . . .

On February 3, 1933, the new Royal Society Mond Laboratory was officially opened at the University of Cambridge by Prime Minister Stanley Baldwin, then also the university's chancellor. The money came from the Ludwig Mond Bequest to the Royal Society, and the laboratory was meant mainly for the development of physics of the advanced type in which Kapitsa was pioneering. The Mond Laboratory was to be actually within the Cavendish Laboratory complex, semi-independent but under Rutherford's supervision. On the main door of the Mond Laboratory, a picture of a crocodile was carved at Kapitsa's request, in Rutherford's honor, he said. He called Rutherford *krokodil* "as a symbol of Rutherford's scientific acumen and career," because "this animal never turns back" but always pushes forward; "the crocodile is regarded in Russia with mingled awe and admiration."

In his personal life Kapitsa was also finding increased stability and happiness; in 1929, in London, Anna Krylova became his second wife. She was the daughter of Professor Alexei Krylov. In the early 1930s she bore Peter Kapitsa two children.

Kapitsa's father-in-law was a prominent mathematician, physicist, astronomer, and above all a first-rate shipbuilder. Although at first in his British residence Kapitsa appeared to be on a Soviet mission, but later ceased this connection and became, in effect, a Russian expatriate, Krylov was never an émigré. Krylov's years in England, 1921–1927, were spent clearly on a mission for the Soviet government: he supervised the building of ships ordered in England by the Soviets and carried out other technical assignments from Moscow. True, he felt independent enough to meet, and eat and drink, with those of his prerevolutionary Russian friends and associates who were now émigrés in London and Paris; he listened to their anti-Soviet talk, but he was most careful and reserved on any problem involving Russian politics. "Krylov had to return [to the Soviet Union]; therefore he had to be cautious," wrote Professor Timoshenko.

Krylov was destined to play an important role in Kapitsa's eventual fate, but there are two different—in fact, diametrically opposite—reports on the nature of that role.

V

It was in the late 1920s and early 1930s that the Soviet government intensified its bold, smart campaign of enticing gifted émigrés back into Russia. Stalin wanted certain key men of the arts and sciences to return. His agents—or just nostalgia—had already won several successes. Among the willing returnees were the composer Sergei Prokofiev, and the writers Maxim Gorky, Alexei Tolstoy, and Ilya Ehrenburg. Some who were sent abroad on missions could have stayed as émigrés, but did not. Among such returnees was Professor Krylov, Anna Kapitsa's father.

And now for Kapitsa. As Peter's renown became worldwide,

Stalin and his men realized the scientist's worth. They now knew that in letting Kapitsa go abroad, a grievous error had been made. Two items were just then discovered by Soviet intelligence men in England.

Item One.   Anna Kapitsa missed her father. Moreover, as her father's letters began to arrive from Russia, she found that she longed also for one more look at her homeland.

Item Two.   Nominally, Peter Kapitsa was still a Soviet citizen. He was refusing all offers of the British government to make him His Majesty's subject.

Why was he shunning British citizenship? Was he now pro-Soviet? No. He was merely a patriot of his old fatherland without any love for the government that happened to be ruling it. He felt it was his duty to return to Russia someday for good—to give to his people the benefit of his talent and knowledge.

Someday, but not too soon. This much was plain from Kapitsa's remarks to his friends on the subject of the Soviets. He would return permanently only if and when there was freedom in Russia.

The Kremlin heard of this, but was still hopeful. In 1933, cautiously, cleverly, the Kremlin let out feelers. Would the prodigal son return just for a visit? A scientific congress was to meet next year in Moscow, surely of much interest to Kapitsa. The congress was to honor the memory of Dmitry Mendeleyev, the great Russian chemist, on the centennial of his birth. It was also known that Kapitsa needed a rest. He could, when the congress was over, take his vacation in the Crimea and the Caucasus instead of the French Riviera. He could bring Anna and his car along, drive anywhere in Russia, then leave for abroad again. His Russian colleagues, from his old teacher Ioffe down to the greenest assistants in Soviet physics, were yearning for a talk with him. Stalin himself gave his word to let Kapitsa out once the visit was completed. Now, would Kapitsa come for a while, a brief while?

Kapitsa shook his head. But Anna pressed, Anna implored. And Peter gave in. Reluctantly, but he did. A Russian émigré, Boris Nicolaevsky, wrote to me about this moment in the Kapitsa's life: "She greatly longed for her native land. . . . Kapitsa himself was very reluctant to go—I know this from his close friends."

VI

Such was one report, one belief, widely current among the Russian émigrés in Western Europe and the United States. Another story, at sharp variance with the preceding, was known less generally and chiefly to those who were scientists and well-acquainted with Kapitsa or at least with his activities.

This second story had it that all through the 1920s Kapitsa went on periodic trips to the Soviet Union and returned to England with no hindrance from the Soviets at all. Kapitsa himself confirmed this when in May 1966, in his address before the Royal Society of London, he spoke of going to the Soviet Union in 1934 "as was my custom." A detailed account was given by Professor Timoshenko in his book of memoirs published in Paris in 1963. Let us turn to Timoshenko's reminiscences.

In July 1926, on a trip to Cambridge, Professor Timoshenko was entertained by Kapitsa "most graciously," as the rather hostile guest conceded.

> He was on the Trinity College staff and had his lodgings right opposite the main gate of that College. To honor my arrival Kapitsa arranged in his flat a tea, to which he invited several young physicists. Kapitsa loved to talk. He told many tales about his trips to Russia, whither he was repeatedly invited to lecture about the development of physics in England. But he was not too burdened by such lectures, and he spent most of his time at Kislovodsk [a resort in the Northern Caucasus]. Now he was talking about his latest trip, during which he had managed to visit his old family home, somewhere in the Volyn Province. At that he had succeeded in carrying out with him a few items of his family's silver, and here he pointed to the tea set standing before us.

But Professor Timoshenko did not believe Kapitsa. ". . . I thought to myself that he had been given this set out of the 'cigarette-case fund'* as compensation for his lectures."

Toward the end of that summer of 1926, while in Paris, Timoshenko ran into Krylov, Kapitsa's father-in-law, on the street. They had dinner in the company of some fellow Russians, and

---

*This expression, "the cigarette-case fund," was then common among Russians both at home and abroad to denote the valuables confiscated by the Communists, in 1917 and later, from upper and middle-class persons in Russia, in many instances before or after their execution by firing squads.

Krylov told Timoshenko that he would like to see him soon alone, on a private matter. Several days later, Timoshenko called on Krylov at his hotel. The matter, it turned out, concerned Kapitsa. "Krylov asked me to warn Kapitsa to decline any further invitations from Russia. . . . At my very next meeting with Kapitsa I told him of this warning, but he paid little attention to it."

Timoshenko saw Kapitsa for the last time in the summer of 1934, at a scientific congress held at Cambridge. Despite his dislike of Kapitsa, he was impressed by the physicist's successes in England. Once more, Timoshenko explained this triumph by Kapitsa's old Russian schooling: "Physics, in its development, demanded large-scale factory-size experimentation, and Kapitsa, with the engineering education he brought from the St. Petersburg Polytechnic Institute, had considerable advantage over the theoreticians of the university type." The two talked about Russia again.

> Kapitsa told me that during his years at Cambridge he had been repeatedly invited to Soviet Russia for reports and lectures, and he found such trips most interesting, since following the reports and lectures it was very pleasant to spend the remainder of a summer somewhere in the Crimea or the Caucasus. I remarked that such journeys were not without their dangers; it was quite possible that one beautiful day the Soviet government might detain him, and he would never return to England. But he only laughed. Such a turn of affairs seemed improbable to him.

Apparently, in returning to Russia in 1934 reluctantly or not, Kapitsa trusted Stalin's word. Why did he?

Some who knew him at the time recall that Maxim Gorky backed Stalin's promise with his own guarantee. Gorky swore to see to it that Kapitsa was not stopped from leaving Russia when ready to go, and Kapitsa believed Gorky because Gorky had secured for Kapitsa his original exit visa in 1921. Moreover, in 1934, Gorky's word was even more effective than it had been thirteen years before. Stalin now openly deferred to Gorky (while secretly plotting Gorky's death, by poison, which came in 1936).

Thus it was, in the early fall of 1934, that Kapitsa returned to Russia, an Englishman perhaps more than a Russian. His friend Niels Bohr, the Danish atomic physicist, accompanied Peter and Anna.

VII

In Russia, Kapitsa looked around with shrewd eyes. He saw that his old homeland was immeasurably stronger and far more orderly than when he had first left it. He was impressed by certain improvements introduced by the Soviets. He was pleased when he reexamined the scenes of his childhood and youth and again when—after parting with Bohr, who sailed back to Denmark—he and Anna drove in their car southward to their beloved Crimea and Caucasus.

But though he and Anna were free in their movements, he noticed that not many Russians were. By the end of several weeks he dreamed of his adopted England, his Cambridge, with its freedom. Naturally, both he and Anna missed their children, and so the two turned back.

They drove north to Leningrad to supervise the loading of their car and of sundry souvenirs onto a Britain-bound steamer. It was here that the Kapitsas were told, "Your exit visas have been canceled."

They were stunned. Their worst fears had come true. Peter argued. In vain. He and Anna had to turn back to Moscow.

In Moscow, high officials were poker-faced. Sorry, but Professor Kapitsa was a Soviet citizen and had to stay. His country needed him. Great things were in store for him. He would have everything—even his Mond Laboratory at Cambridge. Yes, Stalin ordered that, if possible, the entire laboratory in Cambridge should be purchased for him and brought to Moscow. What would the professor say to this?

The professor said, "No." He repeated, "No, no, no," emphatically, again and again.

The officials shrugged their shoulders. They were polite. In contrast to the usual methods of the Soviet police, no force would be used on the great scientist. Give him time, and he would see the light. Such were the Kremlin's special orders. Stalin was patient.

The professor tried to outwait the dictator. For a whole year, Peter and Anna Kapitsa lived in their hotel room, hardly stirring except for a walk, refusing to say "Yes," demanding their right to return to England.

Lord Rutherford and other foreign friends of Kapitsa addressed the Kremlin with protest and plea. The official Soviet answer was "that of course England would like to have Kapitsa and that they, for their part, would equally like to have Rutherford in Russia!" In other words, England had as little right to claim Kapitsa, the Russian, for her own as Russia would have to demand Rutherford, the Englishman, for her laboratories. Four years later, Professor A. S. Eve, the official biographer of Rutherford, appraised this Moscow view as a "sagacious and fair retort."

Rutherford continued trying for a while, nonetheless. He attempted to engage Stanley Baldwin's aid, writing to him on April 29, 1935, "Kapitsa was commandeered as the Soviet authorities thought he was able to give important help to the electrical industry and they have not found out that they were misinformed."

But Stalin knew perfectly well that Kapitsa was a scientist no less than an engineer. He was going to use Kapitsa in both capacities. To Kapitsa, Stalin sent word that he would see him if the professor was in a more placable mood and wanted to talk things over. In time, Kapitsa weakened. He discovered that he longed for his work even more than for England. He would see Stalin. And so the two met and came to an agreement.

Things began to hum. Stalin's new promise was kept. Not sparing the expense, the Soviet government bought and brought to Moscow certain items of equipment in the Mond Laboratory—the items that had been used by Kapitsa for producing high magnetic fields. Rutherford helped in these negotiations most effectively. The British sold these items in the interests of science since no one else but Kapitsa could use this equipment anyway and since the money received for it went to buy England's first cyclotron. The exact British rationale and procedure, in the words of Rutherford's official biographer, were as follows:

> Since Mahomet could not go to the mountain, the mountain had to go to Mahomet. Negotiations were begun and Professors Adrian and Dirac went to Russia to interview Kapitsa and others. Finally the Russian Government bought the apparatus for £ 30,000—a fair and proper price—and Cockcroft had the apparatus packed and dispatched to Russia.
>
> Not all this money came to the Cavendish Laboratory, because the

British Government, through the Department of Scientific and Industrial Research, had contributed large sums for the generator and other apparatus. It was agreed that the Cavendish would not compete with Kapitsa in his field of research, and the money received was devoted to other objects, in the Royal Society Mond Laboratory.

But in time to come Kapitsa was to insist that he did not have a laboratory of his own for the first three or four years after his forcible detention in the Soviet Union in the fall of 1934. The negotiations for the Mond Laboratory equipment may have indeed taken at least two years, and the shipment and installation of the apparatus in its new place in Moscow another year or two.

Much else was done by Stalin for his captive. In 1935, Kapitsa was made director of the Institute of Problems of Physics, within the network of the Soviet Academy of Sciences. A corresponding member of the Academy from his British days (since 1929), he became a full-fledged member of the Academy in 1939.

Yet it was not atomic physics that held Kapitsa's primary attention once he resumed his work. From 1935 on, his major achievements were in low temperatures and their application in the liquefying of air. To his credit he added the first discovery and investigation of hyperfluidity of liquid helium. His small, inexpensive turbine, used to take oxygen out of air, brought him a United States patent as well as new Kremlin honors.

An enthusiastic, devoted circle of colleagues and students formed around him at the institute in Moscow. His Wednesday evening at-homes became a celebrated colloquium for years.

The two Kapitsa children were in time brought from England to rejoin their parents. The Harris tweeds that Kapitsa liked so well were ordered for him. Even the precise brand of Kapitsa's favorite English tobacco was imported for his pipe.

Nonetheless, for a long time he continued to brood, for he greatly missed England and, in particular, Rutherford. Until the very end of Rutherford's life, which was to come in just a few years, the British scientist wrote encouraging letters to Kapitsa at least once every two months. Kapitsa tried to respond with a kind of Russian fatalism. In 1936 he wrote to Rutherford: "After all, we are only small particles of floating matter in a stream which we call Fate. All that we can manage is to deflect slightly our track and keep afloat—

the stream governs us!" Rutherford's death on October 19, 1937, left Kapitsa with a deep sense of personal bereavement.

Meanwhile, in Kapitsa's native land, clouds were gathering, threatening. The purges of the middle and latter 1930s struck Russia in a long, agonizing series. Most of the men and women who had ever had any dealings with the West were arrested and shot or deported to concentration camps. All around Peter Kapitsa, friends, associates, and acquaintances were dragged out of their homes and laboratories to a fate known or unknown. The secret police moved closer and closer to the physicist.

Among others, Lev Landau, a rising Russian star of physics and mathematics, was arrested. A Jew, he was nevertheless accused of pro-Nazi activities. Nearly three decades later, in 1964 (two years after he was awarded a Nobel Prize), Landau recalled with what great courage Kapitsa rescued him by going to Stalin himself and successfully demanding his freedom.

VIII

In the early 1940s, Kapitsa returned to the atomic field by helping other Soviet scientists in their nuclear researches. He built new instruments for the cosmic-ray observations carried on in the high mountains of the Pamirs and Soviet Armenia by the two Armenian brothers, Abram and Artemy Alikhanov. During the war, Kapitsa experimented with uranium and lectured on atomic physics in Moscow's military academies.

And yet the atom did not seem to be his chief concern. When in April 1944, the Franklin Institute of Philadelphia awarded him the Franklin Medal, it was for his work outside the atomic field. For his discovery of hyperfluidity he received the First Class Stalin Prize twice, in 1941 and 1943. Early in 1945, when the Kremlin gave Kapitsa the title of "Hero of Socialist Labor," it was for his researches into the turbine methods of oxygen production.

By 1946, Kapitsa had the Order of Lenin, the highest award in the Soviet scale of honors. At this time, in 1945–1946, he smilingly denied to foreign correspondents that he was under any duress. Urbane and relaxed, puffing on his briar, he spoke in his colloquial English of all the facilities and honors he was enjoying in the land of the Soviets. In his public speeches he dwelt at length on the glories of the USSR. Nevertheless, rumors spread that Stalin was not too pleased with Kapitsa.

Stalin was rewarding him constantly, but more in hopes of spurring Kapitsa on to atomic discoveries than in recognition of work already done. Hints were carried to Kapitsa from the Kremlin: move "closer to actual life" (as the common Russian phrase had it)—that is, closer to the post-Hiroshima reality.

On the news of Hiroshima, Stalin had tripled the salaries of his atomic scientists. As late as December 1945, Kapitsa blandly revealed that his most recent work had been with hydrogen. Unofficially, however, all the world had heard or guessed by then that Kapitsa was leading the entire effort to produce a Soviet A-bomb. Norbert Wiener, who had known him at Cambridge in the early 1930s, said later that he was not surprised. He recalled that in Russia, Kapitsa "became the pioneer of that large-scale, factory-like type of laboratory which had first been employed by [Heike] Kamerlingh Onnes in the Netherlands for low-temperature research, and which is now the standard means of exploring the nucleus and of designing atomic bombs."

In 1945, just as soon as Wiener had first heard of the American bomb, he felt sure that, with Kapitsa training "the Russians in the technique of this sort of laboratory, it would not be many years before they would have mastered for themselves the principles and techniques of nuclear research, whether or not they might capture our secrets by means of espionage or persuade a group of malcontents to serve their purposes."

In the summer of 1946, to Richard E. Lauterbach, a young American journalist who questioned him about the atom bomb, Kapitsa made a wry face. "To talk of atomic energy in terms of the atomic bomb," he said, "is like talking of electricity in terms of the electric chair."

A man of peace, Kapitsa was hoping for an international agreement to outlaw the atomic bomb. He hoped for mankind's survival. Increasingly, he criticized the Americans for what he termed unnecessary stubbornness in safeguarding atomic secrets.

This is where the new mystery of Kapitsa began. Was he sincere in this criticism? Did he gradually allow himself to be convinced by

Stalin's men that we were being perverse in not destroying our stocks of A-bombs as the Kremlin wished us to do and that as a Russian patriot he must do his best for the Soviet version of the A-bomb? Or was he only *talking* like a loyal Stalinist—to cover up his possible decision *not* to lead the Soviet atomic race against the West?

The mystery deepened when suddenly, late in 1946, Kapitsa's name vanished from official Soviet news. He was no longer head of the Institute of Problems of Physics nor in the lists of Russian scientists awarded Stalin's prizes and medals. No letter from him or about him reached foreign parts. Complete official silence surrounded Kapitsa.

Two long years passed, and then in 1948 an article of his appeared in a Soviet journal of experimental and theoretical physics. In February 1949, another article by Kapitsa was printed in the official annals of the Soviet Academy of Sciences. But neither was on atomics—both were on liquids.

Was Kapitsa being *zasekrechen*—that is, surrounded by utmost secrecy and security—because of astounding successes in atomics since late 1946? Or, on the contrary, was he being punished by Stalin because he either could not or would not help the Kremlin's efforts to produce an A-bomb? All sorts of reports circulated then, and still abound now, about this period in Kapitsa's colorful life; but the most authentic facts seem to be these: In Stalin's final years, Kapitsa refused to contribute his genius to the evolvement or improvement of the Soviet atomic and hydrogen bombs. Stalin, not daring to shoot or even exile the great scientist, had him confined under house arrest, which may have lasted several years.

In his *Moscow Summer*, Mihajlo Mihajlov, while reporting on his conversation with the celebrated Soviet writer Vladimir Tendryakov, noted: "Among other things, Tendryakov told us that his friend, the Academician Kapitsa, famous as a mathematical genius, was under house arrest for eight years during the Stalin era." Early in 1965, Ilya Ehrenburg revealed how dismayed Kapitsa's British friends had been on hearing of his arrest. At the end of Stalin's era, Ehrenburg was in England on a mission for the Soviet "peace" movement of the time. He was taken on a visit to Cambridge, where a distinguished physicist and his wife cautiously and unhappily inquired about Kapitsa's troubles. Ehrenburg tried to reassure them; he felt that his hosts "wanted to believe me but did not dare to." They were slightly reassured when Ehrenburg agreed to deliver their gift of a few skeins of wool to Anna Kapitsa (who loved to knit).

That Kapitsa was indeed under house arrest for a period near the close of Stalin's era seems now indisputable, if only because mention of the arrest was later, in Khrushchev's time, allowed to seep through in foreign correspondents' dispatches from Moscow uncensored and unrefuted.

Peter Kapitsa returned to freedom and to the world's headlines soon after Stalin's death. In August 1953, when Russia's possession of an H-bomb of her own became known, Kapitsa's earlier role in this achievement was surmised. In Washington it was recalled that Kapitsa's particular specialty involved the major matter of the hydrogen bomb—the behavior of materials at very high and very low temperatures. Also recalled was a December 1945 statement by Kapitsa to the effect that he had transformed hydrogen into a hard, visible metal. The chairman of the United States·Joint Committee on Atomic Energy once remarked, with disquiet, on Kapitsa's special competence in the technical problems relating to hydrogen weapons.

In 1955, two years after Stalin's death, Kapitsa was reinstated as director of the Institute of Problems of Physics. Also in 1955 he made public his hypothesis about the origin of ball lightning, which in some scientific quarters is seriously considered for its potential as a military weapon of tremendous force.

In July 1957, the British pacifist weekly *Peace News,* in a London-to-Moscow telephone interview, asked Kapitsa whether he had indeed refused to work on Soviet atomic and hydrogen bombs. Kapitsa's reply was, "Quite right," and he went on to reveal that "other Soviet scientists had taken a similar position." This was confirmed in September 1957 by Wilfred Burchett, an Australian Communist, as he described his own visit and interview with Kapitsa "in his palatial offices" in Moscow. He wrote that Kapitsa had said to him, "I have never worked on bombs."

The year was 1957, and much has happened since then. It is quite possible that the party now favors Kapitsa, at least in part, because the scientist has by this time changed his ideas about bombs that are too destructive; it is sometimes supposed in the West that currently Kapitsa at least advises Soviet laboratories concerning the development of atomic and hydrogen bombs and the military use of cosmic-ray energy.

IX

Yet his rebellious voice is still raised, as an outstanding example indicates. Men of science and politics the world over sat up and took notice when on March 26, 1962, the Moscow *Ekonomicheskaya gazeta* printed Dr. Kapitsa's lengthy article "Theory, Experiment, Practice." Therein the internationally famous physicist declared that without the science of cybernetics, Soviet outer space successes would have been impossible. Nevertheless, the scientist recalled, only some eight years earlier certain Soviet dogmatists had denounced cybernetics as something capitalistic and thus worthless.

With dignified anger, Dr. Kapitsa quoted *Filosofichesky slovar'* ("Philosophical Dictionary"), published in 1954, one year after Stalin's death, but still mirroring the official Stalinist negation of computing machines: "Cybernetics is a reactionary pseudoscience, which emerged in the United States after World War II and spread widely in other capitalistic countries as well."

Seizing upon the title of the 1954 book, Professor Kapitsa berated its authors as "philosophers" who had made a "mistake" and who as philosophers should have foreseen the further development of natural sciences instead of pronouncing their rigid judgments on a past phase of these sciences.

Never once did he call them Stalinists. Remarking merely that "this mistake has been corrected," Kapitsa went on to state that already in 1954, if not earlier, Russia's true scientists had refused to bow to those Soviet "philosophers," and how lucky this was for the nation! He wrote:

> Had our scientists at the time, in 1954, obeyed the philosophers, had they adopted this definition [of cybernetics] as their directive for the further development of this science, we can say that our conquest of outer space, of which all of us are justly proud and for which the entire world respects us, could not have occurred, since it is impossible to guide a spaceship without cybernetic machines.

Nor would the Soviets have emerged with their own atomic bomb when they did, Kapitsa continued, had the Soviet "philosophers" been obeyed in their abuse of another science milestone: Albert Einstein's work on relativity. He pointed out that already in Einstein's time physicists had confirmed his theory by their experiments with atomic particles, but that Soviet dogmatists disregarded this evidence.

> To understand such experiments a profound knowledge of the latest physics was needed, but certain philosophers lacked this knowledge. And by now physicists . . . have confirmed the Einstein law, not on separate atoms, but on the scale of the atom bomb. How embarrassed our physicists would have been had they followed those philosophers' conclusions and had they ceased their work on the problem of applying the theory of relativity in nuclear physics!

In his March 1962 article, Kapitsa implied that back in those days, in the 1940s and early 1950s, he was among the bold ones who shrugged off the anti-Einstein mania and the anticybernetic dogma and who went on with their genuinely scientific work. Kapitsa's house arrest may have been caused not alone by his refusal to work on the atomic bomb. An additional cause may have been his disagreement with Stalin's "philosophers" on the validity of relativity and cybernetics.

X

Still, what exactly was behind Peter Kapitsa's sudden attack of 1962 on those Soviet dogmatists for their erstwhile sabotage of Einstein's ideas and computer work in Russia? Why his extraordinary review of this particular Stalinist sin, which, like all the other varieties of the late dictator's whims, was supposed to be safely dead by 1962?

Nine years after Stalin's demise, Einstein and computers were at last raised from the limbo of taboo or official neglect by the Communists. Computers in fact were being extolled all over the Soviet scene. The party's new program, adopted at the Twenty-second Congress in Moscow in October 1961, held that for the next two decades the widest possible use would be made of computing, control, and information machines. Why, then, the outburst by Dr.

Kapitsa—the seemingly belated broadside against those Stalinist dogmatists? Was it merely historical, a proud and near-gloating reminiscence of the sufferings of that horrid period as a prelude to the latter-day triumphs of true scientists?

Not entirely and not primarily. Professor Kapitsa made it clear that the present and the future of Soviet science and politics were involved no less than their past. Interference in Soviet science by Communist politicians continued, he hinted in his March 1962 manifesto. He sideswiped Trofim Lysenko, the leader of Soviet antigeneticists, without naming him, yet plainly meaning him when he wrote about "the incorrect generalizations made by our philosophers, not only in the field of physics, but also in the field of biology."

Kapitsa then proceeded to his main target, which was none other than the Marxist tenet of dialectical materialism. He wrote in his "Theory, Experiment, Practice" cautiously, yet unmistakably:

> . . . Application of dialectics in the realm of natural sciences demands an exceptionally thorough knowledge of experimental facts and their theoretical generalization. Without this, dialectics by itself cannot solve the question. Dialectics is like a Stradivarius violin. To play this most perfect of all violins, one must be a musician and know music. Without this, it would yield false notes just as an ordinary fiddle would.

Somehow he seemed to connect the dogmatists' misuse of dialectics with the fact that young Soviet physicists shunned experimentation. Too little experimentation was being done in the Soviet Union even in the early 1960s, Professor Kapitsa asserted in his significant article. In this lag he saw a danger signal for the future of Soviet science. He explained; he cited facts and figures: as editor of the journal *Eksperimental'naya i teoreticheskaya fizika*, he noted that in the themes of articles submitted to him, those on theoretical physics outnumbered those on experimental physics three and even four to one. For various reasons, "young Soviet college graduates . . . want theoretical, not experimental, work as their specialty," he pointed out. He also warned, "We cannot permit any lag in experimental physics, for this would greatly hinder the normal growth of our physics—would prevent it from occupying leading positions in the world's science along the entire front of most important researches."

Whereas some of the reasons for the young Soviet researchers' reluctance had nothing to do with politics, others did. Professor Kapitsa intimated that fear of Marxist dialectics was among the handicaps to experimentation in the Soviet Union. In sum, he blamed the Soviet "philosophers," who, although less pernicious than they had been in Stalin's time, were still strong enough to oppose true science.

XI

In December 1964, in a speech subsequently published in an Academy journal, Kapitsa called for greater freedom for Soviet scientists when he said that although they could get money for their research more easily than their American colleagues could, the governmental restrictions made Soviet research less productive. Let us emulate some of the American practices, he urged. Availability of able researchers, rather than the attraction of this field or that to the government, should be the guiding principle. Funds should be given to those who can use them fruitfully, not to those in an area of research that may be judged important by the authorities, but that may lack truly capable scientists.

At about the same time, in April 1965, in an oblique but again unmistakable way, he demanded freer travel abroad for those Soviet scholars who really needed it, among them himself. He made this demand clear in his article commemorating the two-hundredth anniversary of Mikhail Lomonosov's death, wherein he praised "the . . . international friendship of scientists" and pointed out: "Nowadays the necessity of personal contacts among scientists is taken for granted by our and foreign savants."

This was, doubtless, to call the world's attention to the fact that ever since 1934 he, Peter Kapitsa, had not once been allowed to go abroad. It was also to ensure the Soviet government's permission for him to travel to Denmark the very next month, in May 1965, when he was to receive the Niels Bohr International Gold Medal awarded to him by the Danish Engineering Society for his work in the peaceful uses of atomic energy.

On May 23, for the first time in thirty-one years, Kapitsa left Soviet soil—to receive the medal from the hands of King Frederick

IX, to tour Danish laboratories, and to deliver a lecture in Copenhagen on high-energy physics.

Finally, in the spring of the following year, he revisited his beloved England. He found his old Cambridge house; he walked through the Cavendish and Mond Laboratories with a considerable heart tug, no doubt; he greeted the few old friends who were still alive. On May 4, as he faced journalists at a Royal Society news conference, he calmly jested about the surest way to bring peace on earth: "Arrange an exchange of scientists from military institutions. Then there would be no more secrets." He regretted the American drain of British scientists, but said it was not a Russian problem "because we have nobody to drain." When asked whether in 1934, on his detention by Stalin, he had felt scientifically isolated, he quizzically remarked that this was "a romantic question." On May 17 he addressed the Royal Society with his reminiscences of Lord Rutherford.

In the fall of 1969, for the first time in their lives, Peter and Anna Kapitsa visited the United States. In his mid-seventies, he looked frail and tired. The visit was limited to just a few campuses and laboratories. He spoke hopefully of Andrei Sakharov's thesis of convergence of America's and Russia's cultures, but his remarks were few and not exactly spontaneous. Rather, they were in answer to some journalists' prodding.

To return to the question raised at the opening of this essay: How much of a center or symbol of opposition to Communist obscurantism is Peter Kapitsa? The answer is that at his advanced age not too much can or should be expected of him. Through the darkest era of Stalinism he preserved at least a spark of the scientist's independence. In the easier post-Stalinist years he has served as a rallying point of resistance to the political bosses. As neo-Stalinism lowers its discouraging curtain on the intellectuals' freedom in the early 1970s, he is still the very much alive conscience of those ever-growing and continually stirring Soviet laboratories and lecture halls. But younger men, such as Andrei Sakharov and the two Medvedev brothers, will have to carry on with a yet bolder course of scholar's freedom and people's advocacy.

PART II
The Academy, Old and New

8. THE SANCTUARY OF SCIENCE

IN no other state and society does a learned body occupy the exalted summit that the Academy of Sciences enjoys in the Soviet Union. In 1925, on the 200th anniversary of its existence, the Academy was legally proclaimed by the Soviet government "the highest learned institution of the USSR"; but long before that declaration, in almost any year of the preceding centuries, the Academy had stood at the head of Russia's academic effort and production. Nor has its importance diminished in the decades since 1925.

And yet, at no point in its history—except perhaps for the brief few months in 1917 between the fall of the czarist government and the rise of the Communists to power—was the Academy of Sciences truly free and independent. Created by the czarist state, inherited against the Academy's will by Lenin's government, it was always a privileged prisoner of the sovereigns and the commissars.

The preceding chapters of this book have given the reader occasional glimpses of the Academy's role. The time has come now to present a brief but consistent account of this singular institution from its birth to our days.

II

In the 1700s, even as he was busy fighting the Turks and the Swedes, Czar Peter I thought of creating in his new capital, St. Petersburg, his "window into Europe," a collegium of savants along Western European lines. In the words of Professor Kapitsa, the czar-reformer "while visiting Western Europe, at once comprehended the importance of science for the development of any country" and so "could not fail to understand that Russia also needed science to become a front-rank, civilized land." The necessity of establishing a Russian academy was discussed during his Western European travels in the celebrated meetings and talks between Czar Peter and the great German scientist Gottfried Wilhelm von Leibniz. The same idea was broached in Peter's correspondence with the German philosopher and mathematician Christian Wolff.

In 1714 a Western European journal published the first mention of Peter's intention to found an academy. In 1717, while in Paris, the czar visited the French Academy of Sciences and became one of its members. In 1718, Peter wrote his first terse unofficial resolution on this subject: "Establish an academy." That year his bitter antagonist Charles XII of Sweden fell in battle, but it took three more years for the Swedes to acknowledge their defeat. The long Northern War came to its end in 1721, and still Peter was busy expanding and shoring up his empire. It was only in 1724 that he issued the final official decree establishing the Academy.

It opened in 1725—nine months after Peter's death. There were as yet no Russian luminaries to staff the Academy; so foreign scholars were invited at good salaries and with other emoluments. Two of them were stars of the first magnitude.

Daniel Bernoulli, a Swiss scientist, came to St. Petersburg in 1725 at the age of twenty-five and stayed till 1733, when he left Russia. He did research in mathematics, physics, mechanics, hydrodynamics, physiology, and medicine and contributed to the Academy's publications until 1778.

Even more famous was Leonhard Euler, the Swiss mathematician, who was only twenty when in the spring of 1727 he came to St. Petersburg to join Bernoulli, the son of his old and famous teacher Johann Bernoulli. In his long and astonishingly productive life,

Euler contributed to every field of mathematics and also to optics, astronomy, hydrodynamics, and acoustics. He was the originator of mechanics as a branch of pure mathematics, the first expositor of the calculus of variation, the inventor of topology and nonquantitative geometry, and the author of the first textbook on analytic geometry. After him were named Euler's formula, Euler's line, Eulerian number, Eulerian variables, the Eulerian constant, and the Eulerian equation. He was at the St. Petersburg academy until 1741, when he left for Berlin; but he came back to Russia and the Academy in 1766 to stay till his death in 1783. He gave Russia and the Academy a total of thirty-one years; but even in the quarter century he spent in Berlin, he never ceased his contact with the Academy in St. Petersburg, continuing on its honorary roster and doing much of his research for its program.

By far, not all was lofty science and glory at the new Academy. There were also pettiness, strife, and squabbles. At all times, a special academician had the duty of composing odes in praise of the current czar or, more often, czarina to commemorate coronations, birthdays, and weddings of imperial persons as well as victories of the Russian arms over foreign foes. The great Lomonosov, too, had to write such odes, not that he really protested. He liked to exercise his versifying talent; and poor as he was, the generous honoraria for the solemn poems were indeed welcome. For one such laudatory poem, Lomonosov received from Empress Elizabeth (daughter of Peter I) the sum of two thousand rubles, equal to his three years' salary at the Academy, which was 660 rubles per annum.

Other academicians were ordered to make up horoscopes for high persons at the court. When Empress Anna wished to amuse herself with a winter carnival, academicians had to help design the famous Ice Palace in St. Petersburg. An ethnographic masquerade accompanied the carnival around the Ice Palace, and at least here the academicians did not lower themselves when they aided in bringing to the capital representatives of all the nationalities, in their colorful costumes, then inhabiting the Russian empire. Actually, one academician tried to make a creditable scientific job of building that palace entirely and sturdily of ice. His success was indeed remarkable.

Germans continued to dominate. Not only professors and their assistants but even the Academy's cabinetmakers and gardeners were mostly Germans or other West Europeans. Russians on the staff were very few; they were mainly interpreters.

Czar Peter I had left behind a set of bylaws for the Academy that gave its members considerable autonomy, including their right to elect their own president. But the clauses on the autonomy were concealed by Peter's successors from the academicians until 1747. The year before, 1746, witnessed the appointment by Empress Elizabeth of a new president. He was Kirill G. Razumovsky, then only eighteen years old and lacking any education whatever. He was a powerful member of the court and owed his presidency of the Academy (as well as the title of hetman of all the Ukraine) to the fact that his brother Alexei was a lover (and according to certain accounts, a secret husband) of Empress Elizabeth.

Razumovsky headed the Academy for nearly two decades. Busy as he was with the intrigues and festivities at the court, he paid comparatively little heed to his Academy duties. Even before Razumovsky's time, the powerful man who really ran the Academy was its secretary, usually a German.

From the 1720s until 1759 this man was Johann D. Schumacher, an Alsatian who held a degree of Master of Philosophy from Strasbourg, was at one time Peter I's personal physician, and had done good work in organizing the Academy. But once in charge of the Academy, he showed a mean streak; a bureaucratic contempt for the academicians and their needs; a delight in setting one group of savants against another, particularly the imported ones against native Russians; and greed for money. The staff's complaints against Schumacher finally moved the Imperial Senate to order his arrest in 1742; but the investigation by the authorities of his activities bore no result. Schumacher had managed to explain everything away and already in 1743 returned to his post. When in 1759, because of his old age, he finally had to retire, he appointed a relative of his, also a German, as his successor to run the Academy.

The fight between the foreign scholars and the slowly rising Russians at the Academy went on for decades. Lomonosov was the bright hope of the Russian party, and in time with his brilliance and energy he truly acquitted the trust. It was unfortunate that at the Academy, Lomonosov was not destined to meet the two great foreigners he really admired and could possibly have gotten along with: Bernoulli and Euler. As Peter Kapitsa notes, by the time "Lomonosov returned from Germany to St. Petersburg, both of them—first Bernoulli, and then Euler—had quit the Academy. . . . Euler left St. Petersburg three days before Lomonosov's return from Germany." Bernoulli never came back. Euler returned to Russia twenty-five years later—one year after Lomonosov's death.

Russian colleagues and students, headed by Lomonosov, complained of the boorish behavior of Germans of lesser caliber with whom they had to deal, of the Germans' reluctance or inability to lecture, and of their refusal to learn Russian or even French. At the very beginning of Lomonosov's stay at the Academy, there were even fisticuffs in which Lomonosov participated; and at one point, as already noted, he was arrested.

Among the running battles in the Academy all that time was the struggle between the devotees of pure or abstract science on the one hand and those—mostly Russians—who believed in applied science, in technology, on the other. An outstanding member of the latter group was Andrei K. Nartov, who began his career as Peter I's favorite mechanic and who is now, in fact, remembered as Russia's best technical innovator of the first half of the eighteenth century. For twenty years, from 1736 till his death in 1756, Nartov was in charge of a great variety of machine shops and craftsmen's work at the Academy, did engineering jobs—and fought Schumacher. It was he who sparked the Russian minority's complaint that resulted in Schumacher's arrest and temporary eclipse. In 1742–1743, Nartov actually directed the Academy until Schumacher managed to regain his post. Nartov continued his struggle against the Germans with hardly any significant help from his colleagues. At that time, in the 1740s, Lomonosov was too young and inexperienced to be of much assistance to Nartov. But as Lomonosov matured, as he grew in knowledge and acquired self-confidence, more Russians spread their wings along with him; and the factions—Russian and German—finally learned to coexist.

With Euler's return in 1766, with young Catherine II pretending a love for enlightenment, the Academy received a new lease on life and productivity. In 1767, Peter Simon Pallas, the great German naturalist and explorer, came to Russia for his series of voyages and researches of eastern Russia's and Siberia's flora and fauna. This work went on well into the 1790s, a more than worthy continuation of the expeditions of Vitus Bering, the Dane, launched by Peter I.

But the French Revolution frightened Catherine II. She began to suspect all progress. In 1792 she ordered the name of Marie Jean de Caritat de Condorcet, the French mathematician, to be stricken from the roll of the Academy's honorary membership because of his participation in the French events. Her son, Paul I, in his brief reign of 1796–1801, treated the Academy with neglect, if not contempt. The fear of the radical West, which led to the prohibition of importing Western literature as well as to other official anti-Western barriers, hampered Russia's scholars by cutting them off from their foreign colleagues. Only a few academicians remained in St. Petersburg, as Emperor Paul sent most of them to other cities to serve as censors.

III

Things changed when Emperor Paul was strangled by noblemen-plotters in March 1801 and when his liberal son, Alexander I, ascended the throne.

In 1803 a new set of bylaws was granted to the Academy, for the first time in many decades restoring to it the right to study, in addition to the physical sciences, such humanitarian fields as history, political science, statistics, and knowledge of the Orient. The number of academicians was raised to eighteen and of their learned aides to twenty. Most importantly, the academicians were now empowered to choose additions to their ranks on their own initiative and by secret ballot.

Their teaching duties were to cease; the middle school—*akademicheskaya ghimnaziya*—was abolished after seventy-five years of its existence. The crafts and shops, of which Lomonosov and particularly Nartov had been so fond and proud, were finally removed from the Academy, which from then on was to stress pure science, yet with sufficient application of it to Russia's practical needs outside the Academy's walls.

The originally high social position of academicians, as intended by Peter I and, for a time, by Catherine II, was once more restored. In the official table of Russia's ranks, members of the Academy were equal to generals of the army. The lower folk were, therefore, to address them as "Your Excellency," and some indeed did.

But not everything went so smoothly in this new era of Alexander I. The Napoleonic Wars of the time were costly, and little money was available for such civilian luxuries as the Academy. Its laboratories, museums, expeditions, and particularly members' salaries declined. University positions did pay adequately, and some academicians actually left the Academy for university chairs if they could not combine both posts.

In addition to the University of Moscow, founded in 1755, and the old Polish university at Vilno and the German university at Dorpat (in the Baltic provinces), which was started by Emperor Paul, Alexander I established two new ones at Kazan and Kharkov in 1804 and the University of St. Petersburg in 1819. Learned societies of naturalists, mathematicians, historians and others were formed at all these centers. Thus the Academy, although still at the pinnacle, was no longer the nation's only body of knowledge.

The increasing mysticism of Czar Alexander, who toward his life's and reign's end became quite reactionary, had its negative impact on the country's education, including the Academy's role. The Swiss-born mathematician Nicholas Fuss ran the Academy as its secretary from 1800 till his death in 1825. For eight years in this period, in 1810–1818, the Academy even lacked a president. As the emperor grew more conservative, so did Fuss. It was he, as already noted, who saw a sinister influence of the French Revolution in Lobachevsky's use of the meter instead of native Russian units of measurement.

The year 1825 brought the death of both the emperor and Nicholas Fuss. The latter's son, Pavel Fuss, assumed the secretaryship of the Academy and kept it the entire span of the new reign—of Emperor Nicholas I, Alexander I's brother—till 1855. The notorious retrograde Count Sergei Uvarov had been the Academy's president since early in 1818. From 1833 to 1849 he was also the empire's minister of education. A zealous guardian of autocracy, he did his utmost to purge the Academy (no less than the other, lesser establishments in his department) of any suggestion of liberalism. Both Fusses, father and son, aided him in this ardently.

They succeeded in keeping the Academy isolated from life and its turbulence; they made it, in Uvarov's proud phrase, "the sanctuary of science" high above the crass everyday doings of little people. No bold pillar-shaking researches or publications were allowed; yet funds were given to improve the Academy's salaries and to repair or expand its buildings and facilities. Even contact with foreign societies and scholars was permitted, but only within certain limits safe for the conservative structure and spirit of the Russian empire.

True, as we have seen, Lobachevsky's genius was not recognized either before or long after 1856, the year of his death. The idea of electing him to the Academy would have been wild sacrilege to its members and even more so to Uvarov and Pavel Fuss, of course. But from 1830 to his death in 1861, the celebrated mathematician Mikhail Ostrogradsky was a member of the Academy, much to its strength and fame. From 1832 till his death in 1864, Vasily Struve was a member, in 1839 establishing the Pulkovo Astronomical Observatory, which was destined to become one of the world's most important. He left behind him a whole pleiad of descendants, who were mostly astronomers, but some chemists, and nearly all of them members of the Academy. (One of them, Otto Struve, migrated to the United States in 1920, here to head for many years some of our nation's outstanding observatories.)

In the reign of Nicholas I, the Academy was reorganized into three divisions. Physics and mathematics constituted the first division; Russian language and literature, the second; and history and philology, the third. This structure lasted nearly ninety years, until 1927.

In their time, in the membership of the second division, such celebrated writers could be found as Vasily Zhukovsky and Ivan Krylov. Later, honorary members ("corresponding members" in the official appellation) included Feodor Dostoevsky, Ivan Turgenev, Leo Tolstoy, Ivan Goncharov, and Anton Chekhov. In 1889 the first woman was given honorary membership in the Academy. This was Sofiya Kovalevskaya, the world-renowned mathematician.

The free winds of the liberal reign of Alexander II, 1855–1881, should have spelled out a great change for the better in the Academy, but somehow did not. The chief reason was, no doubt, the conservative habits of the majority of the academicians. Entrenched in their posts by election for life, and in turn electing mostly their own kind, they wanted no reforms in the Academy. Its longtime secretary, K. S. Veselovsky, a climatologist, ran the Academy with a steely hand for more than three decades, from 1857 to 1890. Even as a reform of the bylaws was proposed in 1865, he insisted that the Academy be kept aloof from the needs of the nation. The Academy's task, he said, was to think and research; the job of non-Academy Russians was to apply to life's necessities whatever the Academy would discover. At the time, some outraged professors on the levels below the Academy publicly urged the abolition of the Academy as something that had outlived its age. They wanted to transfer all Russian scientific endeavor to universities.

The Academy wouldn't listen. Undaunted, the Academy went on its sedate way. It would not elect to its membership such leading savants as the biologist Ivan Sechenov and the physicist Alexander Stoletov. A major disgrace was the Academy's refusal in 1880 to elevate Dmitry Mendeleyev from honorary to full membership. After the assassination of Alexander II by thoughtless revolutionaries in March 1881, his son and new czar—Alexander III—initiated a veritable rule of repression. Count Dmitry Tolstoy was appointed to head the Academy—and he was at the same time the minister of the interior and the chief of the gendarmerie!

The accession of Nicholas II in 1894 improved matters but little. The Academy was at the apex of Russia's learning, indeed, and some of its members were productive and world-famous, but most of them were conservative in their political outlook: in the affairs of the state and society they would make no unsettling waves. In the 1890s and 1900s such bold prophets as Konstantin Tsiolkovsky would not be even proposed for the Academy membership, less so accepted. The great Ivan Pavlov was advanced to a full Academy membership only in 1907, three years after he had become a Nobel laureate.

A sensational incident causing high indignation among the Russian intelligentsia occurred in 1902. In February of that year, the Academy elected Maxim Gorky, the writer, to honorary membership. Because of his radical views, it was expected by some that Gorky would reject this mark of esteem so as to demonstrate his hostility to the czarist government. But he had no such plan. He liked the distinction, and it was Czar Nicholas II himself who barely two weeks later ordered the cancellation of Gorky's honor by the Academy.

Anton Chekhov, an honorary member of the Academy since

1888, felt outraged. He waited a few months for the Academy to override the emperor's veto. But the Academy accepted the imperial edict meekly. Chekhov spoke to Leo Tolstoy, also an honorary member of the Academy, about protesting. Tolstoy, then in his mid-seventies and more of an ascetic philosopher than the fiction writer he had once been, shrugged it off. He held all this Academy business as so much worldly nonsense. At the time of his own election, he had not even bothered to acknowledge the honor; no, he did not consider himself an academician. He would not protest.

So Chekhov and another writer, Vladimir Korolenko, acted without Tolstoy. In August 1902 they announced to the Academy that in protest against the cancellation of Gorky's honor they were withdrawing from their own membership. Although the two did not seek to publicize their resignation, the news became common knowledge at once. It was a national scandal. Applause for Chekhov and Korolenko was as intense as that year's public censure of the arbitrary czar and the subservient Academy.

IV

When the great upheaval of 1917 came, the Academy was, of course, no less affected than any other Russian institution. The overthrow of the monarchy in March of that year was met by most academicians with equanimity and even cheers. Few among them were convinced extreme monarchists; most were either moderate conservatives or liberals. In May 1917, the name was officially changed from the Imperial Academy of Sciences to the Russian Academy of Sciences. That month, for the first time in its history, it actually elected its own president, Alexander Karpinsky, a geologist of foremost renown, then seventy years old.

As so many well-intentioned Russian intellectuals of that effulgent time, the academicians were full of high hopes for a bright future, now that the monarchy was no more. Their hopes were dashed by Lenin and his Communists. The Red November of that year, with its take-over of the country by Lenin, was met by the Academy in shock and disbelief. The ensuing civil war and famine were particularly hard on those intellectuals who would not recognize Lenin's government. Such intellectuals were many, and the Academy was most definitely among them and of them. By a recent admission of the Soviet historians of the Academy, as late as 1928 there were no Communist party members among the academicians.

Until the spring of 1918, the Academy displayed a sort of low-key resistance to Lenin's decrees, which were also rather mild at first, Lenin, in fact, instructing Anatoly Lunacharsky, his commissar of education, to use "caution and tact" in dealing with the sensibilities of the Academy. But gradually, beginning with April 1918, there was increasing cooperation between the Academy and the Soviet government.

As Lenin carefully, patiently extended subsidies and smiles toward the haughty academicians, he was solving the age-old dilemma of the Academy: to be or not to be practical. His solution was, of course, in favor of that which would pragmatically strengthen the nation and his rule over it—pure science was now most certainly pushed into the background; applied science, technology, came to the fore.

Lenin until his death in 1924 and Stalin throughout his reign till 1953 used the Academy for just such purposes and hardly any other. Particularly for Stalin there were two tasks, immediate and long-range: to bring engineers into the Academy and to make the Academy as Communist as possible.

The engineers were brought into the Academy beginning with 1929. This was the first year of the First Five-Year Plan of Russia's industrialization and collectivization. Here in the Academy, the engineers strengthened in numbers those few scientists who would lower the old kind of Academy prestige by applying their noble formulas to the factory's needs.

It was at this time that Stalin made a special effort to elevate to the Academy minor scientists who, he thought, would be more responsive to him than the old elite. He sent to Leningrad one of his henchmen, Avel Yenukidze, to see and cajole Pavlov into proper balloting. Pavlov tried to be stubborn. As one such candidacy was debated, he publicly complained, "If we admit such scientists to our Academy, it will be not a scientific institution, but God knows what. The reorganization of the Academy is being tackled by individuals who understand nothing about science, who don't know for what the Academy should exist." He sneered about the qualifications of

Yenukidze, even whose name he could not remember; all he could recall was that Stalin's emissary was "a red-haired Georgian." (A few years later Stalin, in one of his spells of distrust, had Yenukidze shot among a number of his closest aides.)

But from 1929 on, Pavlov and his colleagues voted as Stalin told them to. If any scholars were too obstreperous, there were, of course, other measures. Typically, in 1930, Stalin ordered the arrest of some of the country's outstanding historians, including the world-famous Professor Sergei Platonov, who died in exile in the Volga region in 1933 after a year in prison.

It was thus in 1929 that the first Communists appeared in the Academy as its members. These were engineers and lower-rank but ambitious scientists. In 1934 the Academy was transferred from its 209-year-old seat in Peter's capital to the Red capital of Moscow. No more of any safe geographic distance between the Academy and the Kremlin. In February 1936 the Communist Academy, which had been formed by the Kremlin leaders years before, was finally merged with the Academy of Sciences. The purpose was to allow party members who claimed they were historians, political scientists, and philosophers to acquire the high prestige of members of the Academy of Sciences. Not since the time of the eighteenth-century headship of the Academy by the ignorant brother of Empress Elizabeth's lover was the name of the Academy so debased.

The Communist victory and dominance over the Academy was complete. And still Josef Stalin was not sure. With the aid of that amazing fraud Trofim Lysenko, he persecuted and decimated the nation's leading geneticists. The list of these victims was headed by Academician Nikolai Vavilov, who died in January 1943 in Stalin's prison.

Even after Stalin's death, Khrushchev continued Lysenko in official favor, and only with Khrushchev's fall in October 1964 did Lysenko's rule of the nation's genetics cease.

V

Today, rich and prestigious, the Soviet Academy of Sciences reigns—but does not rule. It has sister academies in many a Soviet regional capital. It has hundreds of full members, thousands of corresponding or honorary members, tens of thousands of young adjuncts and assistants. Hundreds of research institutes and thousands of publications are within its far-flung network. Countless delegations and expeditions travel to various corners of the Soviet empire and of the world; numerous conferences and congresses take place under the Academy's auspices or with its active and fruitful participation.

Paeans of praise are sung at home and abroad to the Academy and its accomplishments, but from time to time there is also a sharp voice of criticism by Russians themselves of its shortcomings or even failures in this field of human knowledge or that.

How much actual scientific progress can we total up for the Soviet Union under the leadership of the Academy in the long fifty-five years of the Communist regime? The Nobel Prize is one yardstick of success. Seven Soviet academicians have so far won it.

The very first was Nikolai Semyonov, who was awarded the great honor in 1956, in chemistry, for his work on the kinetics of chemical reactions (sharing the prize with Sir Cyril Hinshelwood of England).

He was followed in 1958 by Pavel Cherenkov, Igor Tamm, and Ilya Frank, sharing their Nobel Prize in physics for their studies of the Cherenkov effect occurring when electrons in water are accelerated to velocities greater than that of light in the same medium.

Next was Lev Landau, whose Nobel recognition in physics came in 1962 for his pioneering researches on gases, particularly for his mathematical theory explaining the properties of liquid helium at a temperature below minus 455.73 degrees Fahrenheit.

Then in 1964 Nikolai Basov and Alexander Prokhorov, researching in quantum electronics, won the Nobel Prize in physics for developing lasers and masers (sharing it with Professor Charles H. Townes, an American, he receiving one-half of the money, the two Russians dividing the other half between themselves).

But the very same prize is cited by some critics of the Soviet regime as proof enough of Soviet inadequacy—of the inevitable result, they insist, of the fetters imposed by the Communist dogma on Russia's scientific progress. Look, they say, only seven Nobel Prizes in the fifty-five years of the Soviet Union, less than one prize for each eight years, whereas the West has in the same period won many times that number!

Moreover, certain Soviet scientists themselves occasionally point out the lags in Soviet science. Peter Kapitsa, for example, is often critical of the state of his country's science even as he lavishly praises it too. In December 1965, addressing the Soviet Academy of Sciences, he pointed out that Russians were behind Americans in "a total of scientific articles in the leading fields of the natural and technical sciences, published by scientists in the main scientific journals of all countries."

He declared, "With about the same number of scientific workers as the Americans we produce only one-half of the extent of scientific work done by Americans." America's expenditures for science grew in 1965 by 20 percent compared with the preceding year, Kapitsa pointed out, whereas the Soviet budget for science in 1966 represented a rise of a little less than 10 percent from the preceding year. He concluded, "In recent times the pace of the growth of science in our country has begun to recede somewhat."

While America continues to attract as permanent settlers some of the best young scientists and engineers from Western Europe, the Soviet Union can boast of no such fresh brain drain from anywhere. The last outstanding Western scientist to defect to the USSR was Bruno Pontecorvo, the atomic physicist, who crossed over in 1950. Even the scientists of the East European satellite countries come over, say, to the Soviet atomic center at Dubna for short periods only, not to stay.

Yet the very emergence and existence of just such scientific centers as Dubna near Moscow or Akademgorodok in Siberia bear witness that Soviet science as led by the Academy is indeed a rich contribution of the Russians to the world's treasury of cultural values.

Again, as in the general problem of the extent and quality of Russia's technical genius, so in this particular question of how good and productive the Academy of Sciences is, the truth lies in between: The Academy is not as glorious as the official Soviet claim represents it to be. It has its deficiencies and lacks, particularly in the limits of freedom accorded to its members; yet Russia's Academy of Sciences does stand for much historic achievement and does hold great promise of future progress.

9. AKADEMGORODOK, THE SCIENCE CITY

"**M**ATHEMATICS!" calls out the Russian bus conductor. "Next stop is biology!"

One truck driver shouts to another: "Take this load of earth over to nuclear physics!"

Notices at street corners read:

Meeting of the Cybernetics Club today.
The English Language Circle is to gather tomorrow.
Don't forget: the Literary Union meets on Friday.

An impressed reporter wrote in the Moscow *Komsomolskaya pravda*: "The ratio of intellect per square meter of this ancient thick-wooded, fierce Siberian countryside is very high, indeed."

The dense forests on the Ob River shores have been cleared sufficiently and the old Siberian reputation for fierceness has receded enough for this new unique city of light to rise—this great science center, the like of which is not to be found anywhere else in the world.

Two thousand miles east of Moscow and twelve miles from the Western Siberian city of Novosibirsk, this remarkable newborn complex has a name of its own: Akademichesky Gorodok, often shortened to Akademgorodok, both meaning "the Academy's little city."

In September 1962, former Sen. William Benton declared, "Its fame and influence will be felt through all of the USSR and possibly through all the world." He had visited Siberia's Science City after telling the Russians that "I had no training in science, and I wouldn't recognize a secret if my nose were rubbed in it!" At the time, it was remarked that this was perhaps the very reason why he had been invited by the Soviet government to see the Science City. Earlier, Ambassador Adlai E. Stevenson and Vice President Richard M. Nixon had been taken to this Siberian site, and they too did not know enough science to spot any secrets here. This was not true of Vice Admiral Hyman C. Rickover, who accompanied Nixon. But then, that was in 1959, when Science City was still in the first stages of building; and not much—secret or otherwise—could yet be seen by any visitors.

In time, Soviet authorities began to resent the frequent Western charge of "Siberian secrecy." To prove that the Science City was not at all out-of-bounds to qualified foreigners, the Moscow rulers increased invitations to Akademgorodok. Thus, already in 1963, in the first ten days of August, the Soviet-American symposium on differential equations was held at the Science City. On the symposium's conclusion, Dr. Richard Courant of New York University, who headed the American delegation of twenty-three mathematicians, was quoted in the Moscow *Sovetskaya Rossiya* as saying, "When I first arrived at the Siberian science center, I was tremendously impressed. Now, after my ten days here, I am simply overcome."

Anyone would be. Already on November 1, 1963, the Siberian Science City counted within its confines one large brand-new university and forty-two truly outstanding institutes of research and teaching. Their combined personnel was close to thirteen thousand, with an eventual goal of fifty thousand employees. The roll call of men and women with learned degrees consisted of nearly one thousand doctors and candidates of sciences. There also were almost fifty academicians. By 1971 the number of academicians had grown to seventy, and there were then some two hundred Doctors of

Science and twenty-two hundred *dotsenty* (assistant professors and lecturers) at Akademgorodok. Back in 1958, just one member of the Academy could be found east of the Urals.

I I

This all began in 1957—the year of the first two Sputniks—when Premier Nikita Khrushchev ordered the Siberian branch of the Academy of Sciences to be established and the Science City to be built on this primeval *taiga* site, bulldozed clear of its thick growth. His aim was to speed up a growth of a far different kind: of science and technology, of industry and urban development—to explore and utilize the vast and relatively untouched resources of this huge domain called Siberia.

Reasons of a military nature played their undoubted role in this step. Science as a handmaiden of Soviet war technology for many years was too concentrated in European Russia and the Ukraine. It was high time to move some of the institutes and laboratories, and start a number of new ones, farther east. It would be safer. Also, from Siberia, Soviet science could serve as a shining lesson to a few assorted Asian friends and foes, particularly to Red China.

Some Western observers, however, always have questioned the wisdom of clustering so much science and technology in one center. Congregation of so many choice brains and machines in one place may be too vulnerable a target in case of war, especially in view of a possible conflict with Red China. Withdrawn far from the West but close to the East, how near a possible theater of war this Science City may yet prove to be!

Few such Oriental daggers gleamed against the Soviets in 1957, when Khrushchev first asked Mikhail A. Lavrentyev to head the project in its embryo. Academician Lavrentyev, then fifty-seven years old, responded with alacrity and gusto. He at once moved from Moscow to Novosibirsk to head the new Siberian branch of the Academy and to pore over the first blueprints of the science center. A topflight mathematician, he was internationally famous for his work on the theory of functions of variables and for his accomplishments in applied hydrodynamics and explosions, as well as for his activities in cybernetics.

Administrator no less than scholar, Lavrentyev found it easy to lead a whole swarm of colleagues and assistants from Moscow, Leningrad, and other centers to the Siberian frontier. Soon there were more applicants than Lavrentyev could immediately use. Young scientists, in particular, were attracted by news of the daring undertaking—by the very idea of the Science City and the breathtaking size of it. As important was the promise of higher salaries and more spacious and modern living quarters. Quick advancement up the Soviet ladder of campus and research jobs was another alluring prospect.

So great was the rush that some academic institutions back home became alarmed and began to complain. They were loth to lose their best men and women to this Siberian novelty, and thus many seekers were told to forget about volunteering for the Ob River frontier.

The stampede to the east found its way into a rather truthful Russian novel. Daniil Granin's *Idu na grozu* ("I Go Against the Storm"), published in 1962, pictured the despair of a group of young Moscow and Leningrad physicists who rushed to sign up for Novosibirsk, only to be rejected because they were needed where they were.

But many did come, and still continue to come, with the result that the average age of the Science City scientific personnel is younger than anywhere else in the Soviet groves of academe.

If any Moscow or Leningrad scientists were romantically lured, or others soberly halted, by the thought of roughing it at the Ob frontier, they were wrong. These days, such large Western Siberian cities as Novosibirsk are long past their pioneering era. True, back in 1896 when it was first founded, this settlement—then called Novonikolayevsk in honor of the young Czar Nicholas II—was not even a town, but just a camp for the workers building the Trans-Siberian Railroad. Soon it was a transit point for land-hungry peasants trekking from the Ukraine and other crowded parts of Russia to start new villages in the fat virgin steppes of Western Siberia.

In both world wars, industries were evacuated to this safe Ob

River shore; and new factories were added. The Soviet era's five and seven-year planning helped, too, until Novosibirsk mushroomed into a giant of a million inhabitants. Turbine-making, meat-packing, and the manufacture of farm machinery are among the city's foremost industries.

Thus, a goodly measure of urban civilization already was here when Lavrentyev and his initial staff came to mingle with the foundation-diggers and bricklayers laboring to erect the "Academy's Little City." What with the engineering and working talent available in Western Siberia and with the priority decreed for the project by Khrushchev, additional manpower and needed material were sent here to build the science center. They keep on streaming, as new institutes constantly are being constructed.

The already completed laboratories, lecture halls, libraries, and housing facilities are a complex of squat, solid, three and four-story buildings, flanked by acres of tall pines, fir trees, and birches. The green wall protects Akademgorodok from the fury of the Arctic winds and cold, yet promises new space for future institutes still to be erected.

The buildings, though recent, are not exactly modern in appearance. They are stodgy, too stolid as well as solid. Certain young Moscow architects say it is a shame that not more imagination was used in designing the Siberian complex—that not more of the glass-and-aluminum aspect was created here. One young Soviet architect expressed her hope publicly in an official Soviet journal that the time yet will come when at least eight of Novosibirsk's institutes will be gathered into a supermodern, airy vision of the latest designs and lightest-looking materials.

The transportation network of the new city has not been planned entirely well either. Bus routes between Akademgorodok and Novosibirsk have on occasion broken down. But on the whole, the utilities and amenities are both sufficient and efficient. To keep up with this human influx, the Ob River has been dammed up at a nearby point to make the so-called Sea of Ob, an artificial lake 125 miles long, now providing power, heat, and light for both the Science City and Novosibirsk. There is fabulous fishing and good hunting in the vicinity, and foreign visitors are overwhelmed by the abundant food at picnic sites belonging to the Science City.

III

The list of sciences in which research and teaching are done in the Science City is long and impressive. It includes nuclear physics and thermophysics; chemistry, organic and inorganic; kinetics and combustion; hydroelectronics and hydrodynamics; automation and electrical measuring techniques; higher mathematics with cybernetics as its significant component; geology and geophysics; genetics and experimental biology; many categories of medicine; all kinds of applied mechanics; and such social sciences and humanities as economics and linguistics, anthropology and history.

Even ancient Russian music is one of the subjects of study in the Science City. On April 4, 1970, the Moscow *Pravda* announced that the Academy's Institute of History, Philology and Philosophy at Novosibirsk had gathered on its expeditions to remote Siberian villages a remarkable collection of sheet music of bygone centuries, from which the exact ways and words of ancient singing are now being researched and restored.

A small section of Akademgorodok, the Siberian science complex. *Tass from Sovfoto*

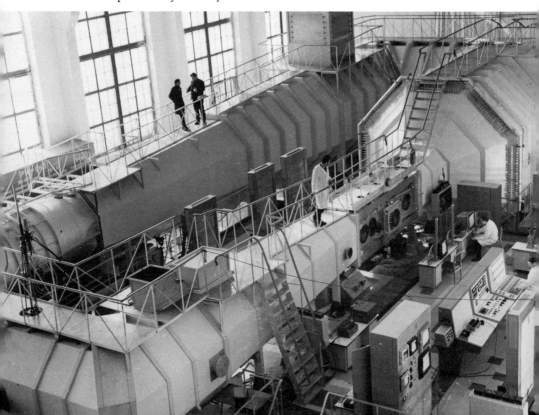

The network of the center's institutes is integrated closely with the University of Novosibirsk, one of the newest in the Soviet Union, but already known far and wide as "the Science University." Its president until recently was Academician Ilya N. Vekua, a Georgian who is a celebrated mathematician. His specialty is the theory of analytic functions of a complex variable as applied to the solution of differential and integral equations in physics and mechanics. He is known particularly for his work in equations of oscillations of elastic cylinders and nuclear shells. The new president is Dr. Spartak Belyayev, an outstanding physicist.

The full Soviet college course is five years long. Students spend their first two years in academic studies only. Their third and fourth years include special work at a nearby institute of their preference. Thus, their gradual introduction to research begins.

During their fifth or final year, the students are occupied at the institute full time, in research either individually or as part of a team. As is the practice in all higher institutions of learning in the Soviet Union, the most gifted of the Novosibirsk student-researchers are asked to stay after graduation as *aspiranty* to higher degrees. Some of them also serve as staff assistants while doing graduate work toward the candidate's rank. The Soviet degree of Candidate is slightly higher than our degree of Master of Arts or Sciences and somewhat below our doctorate.

Much research in the far-flung provinces of Siberia is directed from this Science City on the Ob shores. Some of this may be classed as pure research, while some is applied to, and often connected with, the needs of the mining, industry, and agriculture of the enormous territory. In 1962, one Novosibirsk institute alone sent out ninety-four expeditions throughout Siberia to look for new oil, gas, and other deposits.

Three other Siberian *filialy*, or branches, of the main Academy of Sciences in Moscow—East Siberian, Yakutian, and Far Eastern— are under the official wing of the Novosibirsk branch and thus are supervised also from Akademgorodok. In addition, this Science City has something to say administratively about some two dozen institutes scattered all over Siberia. Among them are the Institute of Frost, for permafrost study, at Yakutsk farther north; the Institute of Vulcanology on Kamchatka; and others in Transbaikalia, Buryatia, at Magadan on the shore of the Sea of Okhotsk, and even on the island of Sakhalin.

IV

To all these institutes, agencies, and other lower schools, a significant call goes out yearly from Science City: "Find the smartest budding mathematicians and physicists among the high school students in every nook and corner of Siberia; round them up; send them down to us by the quickest plane, train, boat, or reindeer. For the great annual Mathematics Olympiad at Novosibirsk will soon be held, and the winners will be rewarded by being kept for their continued education right here, in our Science City."

Lavrentyev says that Soviet educators are against such IQ tests as Americans believe in and go by. "Unfortunately," he wrote in *Komsomolskaya pravda* of August 17, 1963, "these American tests are of little use in the process of finding the best talent for science. The part of ability that is needed for creativity is touched by IQ tests only superficially."

The Science City staffers prefer tough mathematical problems and nothing else, and it is not only the right answer that they want from each contestant. Originality in arriving at that proper solution counts for more than just the solution. Only those showing such originality are judged the winners. A typical announcement to young contestants reads: "To be an Olympics winner it is not necessary to solve all the problems. . . . It is enough that you have solved just one problem in an original manner."

Thus, the Russians have two Olympics, one in sports, but another, less known but more important, in science. The science Olympics began with mathematics alone, and no other discipline. After Stalin's death, computer-minded Soviet professors were alarmed that they did not seem to have enough students capable of learning such newfangled things as linear programming.

First in Siberia, then all over the Soviet Union, professors beat the bushes for promising mathematical talent. Academician Sergei L. Sobolev, chief of the Institute of Mathematics in the Science City of Novosibirsk, set out some years ago to travel up and down the roads and rivers of Siberia seeking gifted youngsters. In many high schools, he informally examined graduating seniors in mathematics. He offered problems of varying difficulty and would single out those who seemed to solve them with ease. Then he would return to give oral tests. The best students would get from him letters of recommendation easing their enrollment in the University of Novosibirsk.

Within a year, his institute took formal charge of the Olympics in mathematics. Now his colleagues and his best students travel, organizing more contests. The Olympics have spread to European Russia, with Math Olympics centers in Moscow, Leningrad, and Kiev. Boys and girls of uncommon ability compete also in physics, chemistry, and biology.

Dr. Sobolev and the other Siberian professors, however, were not the real pioneers. The idea was suggested by a few Leningrad mathematicians in 1934. The next year, the mathematicians of Moscow emulated it, but participants came from Leningrad and Moscow only. The Second World War ended the promising beginning. Some of the best winners perished in the holocaust. Years later, the Siberians remembered the experiment of the 1930s and expanded it greatly by recruiting gifted youngsters actively, persistently, often ingeniously.

The ability was there, the professors argued, only it was hidden or dormant. As a nation, the Russians are mathematically capable. Was the Russian addiction to chess a symptom of mathematical ability? A Russian mathematician disagreed: "Chess akin to mathematics? Wrong. Chess is played by two opponents who hamper each other, with each move disrupting the other's harmony of logical thinking. Rather, mathematics is closer to music. In music, as in mathematics, you cannot remove a single link without crippling the whole. Both are equally fragile, transparent, emotional. The solution of a problem excites a person no less than music excites its performer or listener."

The Olympics procedure is this: Each October, the Soviet press, particularly *Komsomolskaya pravda* and other newspapers for youth, publish a series of problems offered by the All-Union (National) Correspondence Olympics in physics and mathematics, as well as chemistry and biology (the last two subjects were added rather recently). The deadline for sending the answers to the main universities in the fifteen Soviet republics is December 1. The winners of these Olympics-by-mail are invited to come to their regional capitals to compete. In these contests they meet other boys and girls, winners of the in-person (not by-mail) contests already held. From these groups, finalists are selected for the very last Olympics on the all-Soviet-Union level. The best of the winners are transferred to a special high school, which practically assures their acceptance into an elite university, either as special or regular students.

V

The Siberian winners in physics and mathematics are housed first in a summer Science Camp at Novosibirsk, with a program of both recreation and study under young scientists—*aspiranty* and assistants from Science City—who volunteer for these tasks.

In the fall, the students are transferred to a special mathematics-physics high school maintained since 1962 at Science City, where again, in addition to regular teachers, young Novosibirsk scientists volunteer as special lecturers or experiment-supervisors. The school is called *Internat* Number 165.

The school has its own Cybernetics Club, which meets on Fridays for discussion laden with all sorts of weighty problems. Recently, the evening's agenda included a debate on the problem of esthetic education for the young. The Moscow *Literaturnaya gazeta* reported that those present "expressed quite a few ideas, some naive, and others serious."

So contagious is the example of Internat Number 165 that other schools in Novosibirsk proper also emphasize mathematics and technology. Youngsters of Novosibirsk's various schools are the only ones in the whole Soviet Union to have a Club of Young Technologists that is coordinated through a special television program of the "do-what-we-do" kind. This means that one group of members builds a piece of equipment in the television studio under cameras and with proper narration. The audience, mostly club members, try to do the same in basements, attics, and school shops. The club was founded in October 1961 and now has a wide circle of admirers and practical followers, including college students and army-rank hobbyists.

Special *internaty,* or privileged boarding schools, for ninth and tenth-grade children "gifted in the area of mathematics and physics," were organized in 1963 also in Moscow, Leningrad, and Kiev. A typical Olympics contest was reported from the Smolensk region in western Russia in August 1969. Here in a pleasant camp, a summer school was run for two hundred eighth and ninth-grade winners of the previous Olympics in physics and mathematics on the city, county, and provincial levels. By the end of the summer session, the most gifted of the two hundred had been selected to go to the special schools of the regular academic year at the University of Moscow and the Smolensk Teachers' College.

Each such school has about 360 pupils drawn from different regions. Each school is affiliated with a university, which contributes professors to the school's teaching staff. The University of Kiev details to its high school nineteen professors and ten instructors— one teacher for each five pupils. Team teaching is often used.

When a pupil enters the university, a professor works out an individualized program of college-level studies for him. It has to be individualized because in his special high school classes the talented student has completed some college courses.

Outstanding stars of Russian mathematics, men with international reputations, give generously of their time to schooling winners of the Olympics. Among the celebrities volunteering is Academician Andrei N. Kolmogorov, Russia's foremost authority on the theory of probabilities. He teaches gifted youngsters in a suburban Moscow high school and has worked out a special program of higher mathematics for the junior-class teenagers. A girl student delightedly declared that higher mathematics was actually more interesting than the elementary math that she and her classmates had studied in their earlier classes.

One Soviet mathematics professor was frank: "Sure, I want excellent students in my college courses. Usually, I look for promising material among college freshmen, but I'm greedy. I cast my net among the youngsters two years short of college age." He began his selection of capable mathematicians as early as the junior year of high school. He delivered guest lectures—at no pay—in several schools. He drew into his effort as many as eighteen volunteer assistants to lecture, to examine, to select, and to encourage the gifted ones.

In March 1965, at the University of Novosibirsk nearly one-third of its freshmen who specialized in mathematics and physics were winners of the Olympics. Younger and yet younger pupils come to the Olympics. One of the Siberian winners was twelve years old. By far fewer girls than boys are winners. While the winners get the main prizes, the nonwinning participants receive certificates of honor and prizes. High schools and teachers who prepare a more than ordinary number of participants are given their own honors.

Some remarkable cases of talent unearthed in rural areas are reported. A boy from the Pacific Ocean island of Sakhalin, Boria Tsikonovsky, had completed only five grades of his school when he took part in the third round of the 1965 All-Siberian Chemistry Olympics. The contest had a maximum of twenty-five points, but he won fifty—he solved each of the five problems in two different ways. A Soviet mathematical marvel, Pavlik Pankov, finished in one school year (1964–1965) all four grades of high school and won a gold medal. He was only fourteen when in 1965 he entered the Kirghiz State University in Frunze. By the spring of 1966, he had completed basic courses of the university's first two years.

Other winners, students at the University of Novosibirsk, may not be sure whether they are freshmen or sophomores; that is, officially they must be freshmen; but they have passed all freshman courses, have certain basic second-year university courses behind them, and are already working in some third-year courses. After just one year at the university, a few of the Olympics winners wrote monographs on theoretical cybernetics, which were published in the university's learned journals.

There are occasional protests against this emphasis on the exact sciences. What about humanities and the social sciences? Demands for special Olympics in literature have been heard, but little heed has been paid them. When an Olympics in humanities was tried by the professors of structural and applied linguistics at the University of Moscow, mathematically gifted youngsters predominated.

Proponents of the precise sciences insist that youngsters in the special math-and-physics schools are given necessary courses in humanities and that they are encouraged to participate in art, music, writing, and dramatics. Opponents are not convinced.

There have been charges that winners of the precise science

Olympics are pampered and become spoiled brats. A Moscow teacher grumbled, "These Olympics only corrupt our pupils. Each participant decides he is a genius; and when he wins, oh my, there is no end to his narcissism!"

Olympics winners are accused of disdaining menial effort, even in emergencies. One case was reported where during a rainy spell, the roof of the Novosibirsk school sprang a serious leak; a woman employee rushed into an Olympics winner's room, shouting, "Get pails and rags! Call all the fellows!" The winner, with Olympian calm, pronounced, "I have no time for this. I am studying."

It is also said that some attempt to rest on prior laurels. One announced that he was not "in a mood" to take any more examinations. He went on a pleasure trip instead of reporting for a test. He was expelled. Eight of twenty-nine winners in this group were expelled for similar antics.

Friends of the scientific Olympics argue thus: In ordinary schools with slow or unoriginal methods, talented youngsters are neglected and even retarded. If not found through these contests, gifted boys and girls are lost to Soviet science.

Occasionally, a winner fails the entrance examinations to an engineering college. In engineering, memorizing is more appreciated than original thinking. A professor who has recommended an Olympics winner is outraged when he hears of his favorite's failure. He protests vigorously, but the examiners reply, "You have trained him to be a scientist; what we want is an engineer."

By now millions of pupils participate in the scientific Olympics. Winners going on to college and postcollege careers are counted in the thousands. Mathematics is far above physics and chemistry and far, far in front of biology.

VI

Foremost among the originators of these Olympics and the most passionately propagandistic of all the Soviet mathematicians, Academician Sobolev proclaims that mathematics is the "singular cement" uniting all sciences. To objectors, he and other Soviet professors piously quote Karl Marx himself: "A science reaches its perfection only when it succeeds in using mathematics." Sobolev is never tired of proclaiming that mathematics is the queen of all sciences, binding all sciences into one harmonious entity. Cybernetics, to him, is the unifying force par excellence. Sobolev speaks of the "mathematization" of all sciences via his batteries of electronic computers.

Indeed, in Siberia's Science City, mathematics and physics are being studied not only by the practitioners of the precise sciences, but also by economists, linguists, and the like. To a session of the Learned Council of the Social Sciences at the Novosibirsk University, a varied group came to hear Valentin A. Ustinov defend his candidate-degree thesis on "Certain Problems of Applying Electronic Mathematical Machines in the Science of History." This was the result of Ustinov's part in a Soviet research team that used computers to decipher a batch of Mayan inscriptions. His listeners, opponents, and applauders included archaeologists, historians, anthropologists, ethnographers, linguists, and, of course, mathematicians led by Academician Sobolev himself.

Thus, this Siberian Science City refutes the charge sometimes advanced by Western critics that Soviet science is too compartmentalized, that there is little communication between its various fields and disciplines. "Not so," say the men and women of Novosibirsk as they point to Ustinov's thesis and to those discussions on ethics and esthetics at the Cybernetics Club.

In this intercultural exchange and fusion, as in so much else, Akademgorodok of the Ob River shores is a leader. A provincial city? Not at all. Although its site is on a periphery, of course, there is travel and other contact between Novosibirsk and Moscow; between it and Leningrad, Kiev, Kharkov, Prague, Paris, London, New York, Chicago, and San Francisco. The unprecedented Akademgorodok is very much alive by now in the minds and mails of the world's outstanding authorities in many learned fields.

And although by 1973 the post-Khrushchevian restrictions by the Soviet government had considerably lessened the exchange of visits between Russian and Western scientists, it is, nevertheless, known that between twenty and twenty-five foreign savants still come annually to this Science City in Siberia.

10. WHAT HOPE?

ALTHOUGH Akademgorodok is no longer secret or hidden, if ever in its existence it was that, there are in the Soviet Union certain other research towns that are completely wrapped up in mystery. No foreigners and very few Russians are allowed to visit them. No one is permitted to talk, even less write, about them.

But a Soviet journalist did have a glimpse of one such town. Later, he defected to the West, and in 1968 he published a frank and thoughtful book about his former country. In this book, *The Russians*, Leonid Vladimirov writes, among other things, about his visit to the scientific town, which, like Akademgorodok, is situated in Siberia, but is so secret that it is not even shown on the Soviet Union's map.

Vladimirov writes: "It does not have a name, only a number, and if you should wish to send a letter to someone living there, you would have to address it to one of the larger Siberian cities, adding that special number. The people who live in this secret town have given it, among themselves, the name of 'Kitezh.' This is a name borrowed from Russian folklore, where it describes a town cut off from the rest of the world by an impenetrable bog." One day, through his high and intricate Moscow connections, Vladimirov succeeded in entering "Kitezh" and spending several hours there, from noon to nine in the evening. "It was not a long time, but enough to make the experience the most striking of my entire life."

That day, one contact leading to others, Vladimirov found himself the center of a discussion group of young scientists, most, if not all, of them employed on this secret project by the Academy and so enjoying all its comforts and even luxuries, some imported from abroad for the Academy by the Soviet government when the Kremlin uses the Academy for such high-priority secret projects.

Establishing their trust in Vladimirov, these young scientists discussed politics with total candor. They were against the Soviet regime, but they were not for a violent revolution. "These men were not talking about the kind of revolution that would lead to sudden strife, resulting in chaos, bloodshed, and death. They were all quite aware that Russia had already suffered enough in this century from revolution, famine, and war." What they wanted was a change for the humane and the rational *within* the existing system.

Moreover, the change had to be scientifically worked out, for they were not only humanitarians—they were scientists. Vladimirov wrote: "These men, dealing professionally with facts, tended to be bothered, even appalled, by the obvious waste, illogic, and disorder that they noted in 'the way things are.'" They felt that the post-Stalinist relaxations of the Communist regime were not enough and that even these were being taken away by the neo-Stalinists. The young scientists did not exactly cherish the Khrushchevian concessions, which proved so inadequate and fragile. "Their criticism went beyond the customary humanitarian objections to the manifest cruelties of the regime. The time had come, they said, to apply some intelligent scientific analysis to the status quo."

Most of them being members of the Communist party, they meant to work for the change within the political apparatus of the party and the Soviet government and gradually take the political and economic reins away from the ignorant bureaucrats. The change would be slow; "a transitional stage would be necessary, a period in which the country would be governed on the basis of directly scientific decision."

II

This dream of scientists taking over from politicians en route to a more rational and just way of life for everybody, to a rule of peace and happiness, is not so recent and not exclusively Russian.

There was, in the fifth and fourth centuries before Christ, the Greek philosopher Plato, whose *Republic* was to be led by philosophers. In 1643 the Italian writer Tommaso Campanella presented his vision of the semimystical, semiscientific *City of Light*. Even more remarkably, both Sir Francis Bacon of England with his *New Atlantis* of 1627 and Marquis de Condorcet of France with his great philosophical work of 1795 on human progress proclaimed a future reign of scholars or scientists as a practical possibility.

In the early part of the nineteenth century, Count Claude Henri de Saint-Simon predicted, or at least advocated, a rule of engineers and scientists over a future socialist state. One hundred years later, beginning with his *Anticipations* in 1902 and continuing with various other writings, H. G. Wells foresaw a rule of science, a world run by "functional" men, all holding some sort of advanced professional degree.

In the early 1960s in the Soviet Union—to some highly placed members of the Academy at least—it appeared as if the dream were coming true. Said Academician Lev Artsimovich, the well-known atomic physicist and the Academy's secretary, while speaking to an American journalist in the fall of 1963 at a Pugwash conference, "We are voluntary advisers to our political leaders. We have one or two good features. We have a comparatively high degree of honesty. That comes from our scientific style of thinking, which is carried on without reference to the opinions of other men. And we are comparatively independent, which also comes from our scientific training. . . . I think we are better educated than politicians. . . . We know better than anyone else what there is to be concerned about. . . . There has been a sudden surge for us to levels of high importance."

The academicians' advice to Khrushchev was on the side of the angels—the side of peace. They thought they were slowly but surely succeeding in influencing the Communist party and its government toward more concessions to the people, toward a more cautious foreign policy of less aggression and more genuine friendship for the peoples of the world. The party seemed to be in retreat before the scientists' gentle push: in the early 1960s the party by special decrees acknowledged that certain scientific-research institutes were to be free of the party's control. It appeared at the time that the tide was thus turning—that Soviet scientists and researchers were beginning to use their newly won freedom, tentatively and tenuously, to emerge from their laboratories, lecture halls, and campus offices into the state's councils.

The dream did not last long beyond Khrushchev's ouster by Brezhnev and Kosygin in October 1964. As the former Soviet journalist Leonid Vladimirov puts it so well, in these neo-Stalinist days the Academy of Sciences is still "the single most influential group of men in the entire country"—but its influence is not political. "As long as they keep their noses firmly to their test tubes, they may walk through their lives on a red carpet that stretches invitingly through years of honor and privilege."

And yet the very same year in which Vladimirov's appraisal was printed, in 1968, a Soviet academician proved that not all of the scientific elite would keep their noses to the tubes meekly. I refer to Academician Andrei Sakharov and his unprecedented activity.

III

Andrei Dmitriyevich Sakharov, fifty-two years old in 1973, is a nuclear physicist. Until recent years, so secret was his work that the Soviet government did not permit much information about him or his achievements to reach the outside world. We knew, however, that in 1950, together with Academician Igor Tamm (later a Nobel laureate), Sakharov proposed the utilization of electric discharge in plasma located in a magnetic field to obtain controlled thermonuclear reactions. In 1958 he attended the second International Atomic Conference in Geneva. A series of his works of the late 1940s and early 1950s on cosmic rays, electrons and positrons, and other such germane areas of physics became known abroad. Finally, despite the tight official curtain behind which much of his research was continually kept, it was revealed that he could be considered the "father" of the Soviet hydrogen bomb, or, at least, one of the few topflight Russian scientists responsible for the invention of that bomb. He has been a member of the Academy of Sciences since the age of thirty-two, an unusually early time to achieve this distinction, since most Russian scholars normally reach it only in their fifties.

A winner of many state honors, he has, nevertheless, refused to be a pet of the Kremlin: in 1968, Sakharov went on record with his sharp criticism of his government's policy. In June of that year he issued a 10,000-word statement entitled "Thoughts on Progress, Peaceful Coexistence, and Intellectual Freedom." In it he castigated the Soviet leaders for their neo-Stalinism, and he demanded that the Soviet people be given complete and immediate freedom of information and discussion. In problems of foreign policy, Sakharov proposed to the Kremlin an immediate cessation of its wasteful hostility to America and of its sowing of disunity and divisiveness in the world. Although criticizing the United States government for its actions in Vietnam, he chided the Soviet government for its policy and activities in the Middle East. Sakharov called on his country's leaders to break with their imperialism and repression. He asked for joint action with Washington in preventing the triple danger of nuclear war, of worldwide famine (predicted by him to begin in 1975–1980), and of the planet's pollution. He urged drastic measures to halt and reverse the latest Soviet process of reviving the worst features of Stalinism.

Academician Sakharov marshaled his facts in the logical, orderly way of a physical scientist. He wrote that he represented not himself alone, but the best—the most alert—of his fellow intellectuals. In the very first paragraph of his statement, he pointed out that his views "were formed in the milieu of the Soviet Union's scientific and scientific-technological intelligentsia." This great ingredient of Soviet society today feels, he said, "much anxiety over the principles and specific aspects of foreign and domestic policy and over the future of mankind." A major part of this anxiety is caused, in Dr. Sakharov's opinion, by the scientists' realization that the scientific method is being woefully neglected by the world's statesmen.

And what is this scientific method in politics? Sakharov explained: it is an approach "based on deep analysis of facts, theories, and views, presupposing unprejudiced, fearless, open discussion and

Andrei Dmitriyevich Sakharov. *Jay Axelbank, Newsweek*

conclusions." Precisely such an approach is necessitated by "the complexity and diversity of all the phenomena of modern life," by "the great possibilities and dangers linked with the scientific-technical revolution" of this historic but hectic time we live in.

Naturally, the Kremlin did not at all like Sakharov's challenge. Of course, it could not be published in the Kremlin-owned press—the only legal press there is in the Soviet Union; so the author of this challenge made it public through what the Russians humorously call *samizdat*, or "self-publisher." The word is a takeoff on *Gosizdat*, the name of the state press. Numerous typewritten copies traveled from one Soviet city to another, from hand to hand among Soviet scientists, engineers, and other bright intellectuals. At the request of the author, the readers reacted with their arguments or agreement to his thesis; and Sakharov responded to the critique in one manner or another, issuing revised editions of his soon-to-be-celebrated brainchild.

The Soviet leaders and their secret police did not dare to arrest Sakharov; he was too important. Indeed, the Communist party needs Soviet scientists far more than Soviet scientists need that party. He was not arrested even after his daring manifesto had finally made its way to the West and achieved worldwide headlines.

Indeed, in July 1968, a copy of the Sakharov document reached the United States, was translated into English, and published. There ensued some discussion of it in America and elsewhere in the Western world. A number of American scientists arranged lectures and symposia on the Sakharov memorandum. It was publicly hailed as the most remarkable, most hope-giving document to come out of Russia in the half century of her Soviet regime. At the Massachusetts Institute of Technology in particular, the Nobel Prize winner Professor I. I. Rabi and other scientists brought Sakharov's thoughts to hundreds of earnest and receptive listeners.

At one such symposium, President Howard Johnson of M.I.T. called Dr. Sakharov's statement "the most important long-range ideas facing the world that one could consider." He declared that if the course suggested by Sakharov is not accepted, "annihilation awaits mankind." He said, "There is no other way out." Professor Rabi pointed out that all Western scientists agreed with Sakharov: "This paper is essentially written by one of us—a physicist, and young . . . in this sense Sakharov is one of us." The world of science and politics must listen to Sakharov because he "like many of us, realizing the potency of science for the destruction of human life and cultural artifacts, seems to have made it his mission to consider almost the whole range of human effort and to develop proposals which, if acted upon sincerely and universally, would lead mankind to a bright future. He spells out the alternatives with force and with eloquence."

Back home, for his unorthodox views and daring appeal, Sakharov was finally punished. The Soviet government removed Sakharov from several of his posts. In particular, he was dismissed from his post as chief consultant to the State Committee on Atomic Energy. Yet more painfully, he was deprived of his job at a top-secret Institute of Physics situated at Chernogolovka, seventy kilometers from Moscow; and he was also forbidden access to the foremost Soviet nuclear research center at Dubna.

A report came out of Moscow that sometime after Sakharov's

appeal had first begun to circulate, the Soviet leaders summoned the physicist to a special meeting at which the high and mighty members of the Politiburo, the Communist party's ruling body and the supreme power in the nation, tried to argue with him. They told him that he was naive and unrealistic. Whether or not Sakharov argued back, we do not know. Whatever the case, he was allowed to go home; he was not arrested. At this writing, he is still not arrested, although the measures described above are still being taken to repress or punish him short of depriving him of liberty.

IV

Nor was this appeal Sakharov's one and only action. On March 19, 1970, he came out with his second statement. This time he was not alone. The new statement bore also the signatures of two other Soviet scientists: Valery Turchin, an outstanding theoretical physicist; and Roy Medvedev, a talented mathematician.

They addressed their statement as a letter to the leaders of the Communist party and the Soviet government—Leonid Brezhnev, Alexei Kosygin, and Nikolai Podgorny. The letter's theme was the domestic situation and the international role of the Soviet Union. The main point was a plea for a thorough democratization of the country and its policy.

The three scientists' argument was that the party and the government should change their policy in favor of democratization so as to save and improve their own socialism. Such democratization, the authors of the letter declared, should be a gradual yet profound process, a logical and consistent action based on a program conceived scientifically.

They pointed to the Soviet Union's growing lag in its technological and economic development, the lag behind the world's levels in national income and productivity of labor. This deficiency, they continued, was particularly glaring in the introduction and use of computers in economy, where the Soviet Union was a whole epoch behind the United States. They stressed the importance of computers; they called the Western, especially American, invention and utilization of computers mankind's "second industrial revolution."

Wherein is the root of the Soviet lag? Sakharov and his friends gave the answer: in the antidemocratic ways of Soviet life established by Stalin and still not done away with by his heirs in the Kremlin. To the authors of the letter, the cure is in a scientific method of ruling the country's economics. This means, first of all, restoring freedom to the Russian people, most importantly to Russian scientists, engineers, and other intellectuals.

The three scientists in their letter offered a concrete plan of fourteen points to be adopted over the next four to five years, which would give the Russian people a wider control over the country's policies at home and abroad, freedom of information and discussion, political rights, reform of education, a fairer deal for the many non-Russian nationalities in the Soviet Union, and other deep changes.

On March 5, 1971, Sakharov addressed one more memorandum to Brezhnev. He protested that his previous proposals of reforms had been left unanswered, and now he added a few new libertarian ideas. Time passed; there was no reply to this communication either. So in June 1972 Sakharov again directed an urgent plea to Brezhnev, entitling it "An Afterword to the Memorandum." Among the new suggestions contained in these fearless papers of 1971–1972 most notable were Sakharov's appeals to the Soviet government to free political prisoners; to stop using insane asylums as places of political punishment; to grant all Soviet citizens their right to migrate from the country; and to begin, together with other governments, organization of an International Council of Experts that would safeguard human rights, disarmament, and ecological conservation all over the world. And again no answer came from the Kremlin.

These papers of 1970–1972 also circulated in those typewritten samizdat copies by the thousand and tens of thousands all over the country. Their impression on the people, if not on the leaders, was unmistakable.

Who are the two other signers of the March 1970 letter? Valery Turchin, a doctor of physicomathematical sciences, is noted for his work at the Physics-Energetic Institute in Obninsk, an atomic-research center in central Russia, as well as at the Academy's Institute of Applied Mathematics in Moscow. Roy Medvedev is not only a mathematician but also a historian; he wrote a book of one thousand pages on the history of Stalinism. Entitled *Let History Judge*, it was not published by the Soviet printing presses, all of them owned by the party and the government; so it was published and circulated by the samizdat. For this and other nonconformist actions, Roy Medvedev in 1969 was expelled from the Communist party (which he had joined in 1956 when the party seemed to go through a liberalizing phase during Khrushchev's attacks on Stalinism).

Roy's twin brother, Zhores Medvedev, made headlines of his own, both in samizdat in the Soviet Union and in the free press abroad. A molecular biologist of note, Zhores Medvedev is the author of monographs on genetics, gerontology, and the biosynthesis of proteins. The typescript of the several hundred pages of his work, *The Rise and Fall of T. D. Lysenko*, which was banned by the Soviet government, was finally reduced to a microfilm and sent to the United States, where an English translation was published in 1969 by the Columbia University Press. In addition, circulating in the Soviet samizdat was Zhores Medvedev's essay "On International Cooperation of Scientists and National Frontiers," in which he complained against the Soviet censoring of the mail and the tight control over citizens', and especially scientists', travel abroad.

In 1969, Zhores Medvedev was dismissed from his research post at Obninsk, and from then on could find no work because of harassment by Soviet officials. On May 29, 1970, he was seized at his home in Obninsk and taken to a mental hospital in the nearby city of Kaluga. To avoid court hearings in certain delicate cases that may become too public, the Soviet authorities declare many dissidents insane; and these individuals are tucked away without trials. Psychiatrists of the state security police can and do certify anybody insane. (This method of decreeing madness, as so much else in Soviet practice, harks back to the worst of czarist times. In 1836, for example, Czar Nicholas I had the philosopher Peter Chaadayev declared insane for having written a probing and disturbing article. For one whole year, a police officer and a government doctor paid Chaadayev daily inspection visits.)

This time, in the case of Zhores Medvedev, the Brezhnev-Kosygin secret police were not successful. A storm of public protest raised by Sakharov, and joined by Kapitsa, Solzhenitsyn, and other

Zhores Medvedev.

notables, made the government beat a retreat. On June 17, 1970, Zhores Medvedev was freed and allowed to go home. To save face, the secret police announced that his liberty was "provisional," that they were reserving their right to recommit the biologist. Undaunted, the Medvedev brothers had two more books published in the West: *The Medvedev Papers, the Plight of Soviet Science Today* and *A Question of Madness.*

V

Brezhnev can demote or dismiss Sakharov, can bother and annoy him but, so far, apparently cannot imprison him. So Sakharov is continuing his bold activities and can even stir up enough commotion to save Zhores Medvedev from the clutches of the secret police.

Not that all the Soviet scientists who dissent and protest are spared arrests or released as quickly as Zhores Medvedev was. It depends on their age and professional achievements. In October 1968 a young physical chemist in Moscow was among the five protesters sentenced to exile or prison. His name is Pavel Litvinov. He is the grandson of the late Soviet commissar of foreign affairs, Maxim Litvinov, one of the founders of the Soviet state. Pavel Litvinov protested against the suppression of civil liberties in the Soviet Union and also against the invasion of Czechoslovakia; and so he was sent to Siberia for five years of exile and hard labor.

Another celebrated name not honored by the Soviet government is that of Alexander Yesenin-Volpin, a young mathematician, the son of the famous Russian poet Sergei Yesenin. For his part in street demonstrations for freedom, he was repeatedly detained, mostly in insane asylums. Finally, in the summer of 1972, he was allowed to migrate from the Soviet Union. He now teaches mathematics at the University of Buffalo.

In the recent trial of eleven Crimean Tatars in Tashkent, Russian Central Asia, we find two defendants representing the Soviet scientific-engineering strata: Rolan Kadiyev, a nuclear physicist, and Izet Khairov, an engineer. Their alleged crime is their protest against the Soviet leaders' refusal to let Crimean Tatars come back home from Central Asia, to which Stalin had exiled this entire nationality.

A number of other young scientists and engineers are now prisoners in Soviet jails, concentration camps, and mental institutions. In 1970 a Leningrad mathematician, Revolt Pimenov, said, "Some time ago, we scholars lost our sense of personal security. For scientific work, one must be certain of tomorrow." Soon thereafter he was arrested and convicted for keeping and reading samizdat literature. The Communist party's official in charge of this case declared to Pimenov, "Your scientific achievements are well and good. But we do still have enough power. Never will there be any concessions at all in the sphere of ideology!" Pimenov replied with fearless words about people's right to freedom.

These are men of courage. In the wake of Pimenov's case, in November 1970, Sakharov and his fellow scientists, soon joined by Solzhenitsyn, formed a "Human Rights Committee," an unprecedented step in the Soviet Union, where governmental committees are the only ones to exist and function. Moreover, the new committee announced that no member of any political party would be allowed to join the committee.

Valery N. Chalidze, a physicist in his early thirties, a Georgian living in Moscow, was one of the founders and main activists of the Human Rights Committee. For two years he was repeatedly harassed by the secret police, yet, daringly, he continued his work of defending those of his fellow citizens who were arrested and otherwise persecuted in violation of their rights stipulated in the Soviet Constitution.

Finally, in late 1972, Dr. Chalidze was allowed to travel to America, at the invitation from the law schools of New York University and Georgetown University, there to lecture on human rights and the dissident movement in the Soviet Union. Early in his American stay, on December 13, two officials of the Soviet embassy in Washington called on him at his New York hotel. They took away his Soviet passport, and announced that by an order of the Moscow authorities he had been deprived of his Soviet citizenship. He thus became a stateless person—a man without a country.

Cleverly, the Soviet government must have decided that, forced to remain abroad, Dr. Chalidze would be less harmful to the Kremlin's policies than if permitted to return home. But Sakharov and others of his like-minded friends did continue in the USSR at their self-imposed task of defending human freedom in the homeland.

So long as such men and women and their spirit live, so long as there are such bold scientist-leaders as Sakharov and his group, there is hope that Russian science can yet be free; and with it the Russian nation, no less than the whole world, can be liberated and survive in peace.

Bibliography

I. History of Science in Russia; Organization of Science; Education for Science

DeWitt, Nicholas. *Education and Professional Employment in the U.S.S.R.* Washington, D. C.: National Science Foundation, 1961.
_____. *Soviet Professional Manpower: Its Education, Training and Supply.* Washington, D. C.: National Science Foundation, 1955.
Fyodorov, Y. *Science in the U.S.S.R.* Translated from the Russian by X. Danko. Moscow: Foreign Languages Publishing House [1963 or 1964].
Korol, Alexander G. *Soviet Education for Science and Technology.* Cambridge, Mass.: Technology Press of Massachusetts Institute of Technology, 1957.
_____. *Soviet Research and Development: Its Organization, Personnel and Funds.* Cambridge, Mass.: Massachusetts Institute of Technology Press, 1965.
Vucinich, Alexander. *Science in Russian Culture: A History to 1860.* Stanford, Calif.: Stanford University Press, 1963.
_____. *Science in Russian Culture, 1861–1917.* Stanford, Calif.: Stanford University Press, 1970.
_____. *The Soviet Academy of Sciences.* Stanford, Calif.: Stanford University Press, 1956.

II. *Soviet Science and Politics*

Ashby, Eric. *Scientist in Russia.* Hammondsworth, England: Penguin Books, 1947.

Fischer, George. *Science and Politics, the New Sociology in the Soviet Union.* Ithaca, N. Y.: Cornell University, Center for International Studies, 1964.

Graham, Loren R. *Science and Philosophy in the Soviet Union.* New York: Alfred A. Knopf, 1972.

_____. *The Soviet Academy of Sciences and the Communist Party, 1927–1932.* Princeton, N. J.: Princeton University Press, 1967.

Huxley, Julian S. *Heredity, East and West; Lysenko and World Science.* New York: H. Schuman, 1949.

Joravsky, David. *Soviet Marxism and Natural Science, 1917–1932.* New York: Columbia University Press, 1961.

_____. *The Lysenko Affair.* Cambridge, Mass.: Harvard University Press, 1970.

Medvedev, Zhores A. *The Medvedev Papers, the Plight of Soviet Science Today.* Translated by Vera Rich. New York: St. Martin's Press, 1971.

_____. *The Rise and Fall of T. D. Lysenko.* Translated by I. Michael Lerner. New York: Columbia University Press, 1969.

_____, and Medvedev, Roy. *A Question of Madness.* New York: Alfred A. Knopf, 1971.

Parry, Albert. *The New Class Divided: Science and Technology Versus Communism.* New York: The Macmillan Company, 1966.

Sakharov, Andrei D. *Progress, Coexistence, and Intellectual Freedom.* Translated from the Russian by *The New York Times.* With introduction, afterword, and notes by Harrison E. Salisbury. New York: W. W. Norton, 1968.

Solzhenitsyn, Aleksandr I. *The First Circle.* Translated from the Russian by Thomas P. Whitney. New York: Harper & Row, 1968.
(This book is fiction; yet it is also a political-historical document of foremost value for its description of prison-laboratories, where Stalin's government kept and exploited many Soviet slave-scientists and engineers. The novel is banned in the Soviet Union in Russian and in any of its translations.)

Turkevich, John. "The Scientist in the U.S.S.R.," *Atlantic Monthly,* January 1958.

Zirkle, Conway, ed. *Death of a Science in Russia: The Fate of Genetics as Described in Pravda and Elsewhere.* Philadelphia: University of Pennsylvania Press, 1949.

III. *Soviet Science Selected by Fields*

Bernier, Lucien. *Secrets of Soviet Science.* Translated from the French by Alan Neame. London: Allan Wingate, 1959.
(Space exploration, atomics, electricity, electronics, meteorology, geography, physiology, and so forth.)

Gilzin, Karl. *Travel to Distant Worlds.* Translated from the Russian by Pauline Rose. Moscow: Foreign Languages Publishing House, 1957.
(On space exploration.)

Kreiger, F. J. *Behind the Sputniks: A Survey of Soviet Space Science.* Washington, D. C.: Public Affairs Press, 1958.

LaSalle, J. P., and Lefschetz, S., eds. *Recent Soviet Contributions to Mathematics.* New York: The Macmillan Company, 1962.

Parry, Albert. *Russia's Rockets and Missiles.* With an introduction by Willy Ley. Garden City, N. Y.: Doubleday, 1960.

Pisarzhevsky, Oleg. *New Paths of Soviet Science: Notes on Latest Research of Soviet Scientists.* London: Soviet News, 1954.
(Astrophysics, history of the earth, the origin of life, physiology, and so forth.)

Turkevich, John. *Chemistry in the Soviet Union.* Princeton, N. J.: D. Van Nostrand, 1965.

IV. *Biographies and Individual Contributions to Science*

Babkin, Boris P. *Pavlov, a Biography.* Chicago: University of Chicago Press, 1949.

Kagan, Veniamin F. *N. Lobachevsky and His Contribution to Science.* Moscow: Foreign Languages Publishing House, 1957.

Kosmodemyansky, Arkady A. *Konstantin Tsiolkovsky, His Life and Work.* Translated from the Russian by X. Danko. Moscow: Foreign Languages Publishing House, 1956.

Kudryavtsev, B. B. *The Life and Work of Mikhail Vasilyevich Lomonosov.* Moscow: Foreign Languages Publishing House, 1954.

Leffler, Anna C. *Sonia Kovalevsky, Biography and Autobiography.* London: Walter Scott Ltd., 1895.

Leicester, Henry M., tr. and author of an introduction. *Mikhail Vasil'evich Lomonosov on the Corpuscular Theory.* Cambridge, Mass.: Harvard University Press, 1970.

Menshutkin, Boris N. *Russia's Lomonosov: Chemist, Courtier, Physicist, Poet.* Translated from the Russian by Jeanette Eyre Thal and Edward J. Webster under the direction of W. Chapin Huntington. Princeton, N. J.: Princeton University Press, 1952.

Metchnikoff [Mechnikova], Olga. *Life of Elie Metchnikoff* [Ilya

Mechnikov], *1845–1916*. With a preface by Sir Ray Lankester. London: Constable, 1921.

Parry, Albert, tr. and ed. *Peter Kapitsa on Life and Science*. Addresses and essays collected, translated, and annotated with a biographical introduction. New York: The Macmillan Company, 1968.

Pisarzhevsky, Oleg N. *Dmitry Ivanovich Mendeleyev, His Life and Work*. Moscow: Foreign Languages Publishing House, 1954.

Polubarinova-Kochina, P. *Sophia Vasilyevna Kovalevskaya, Her Life and Work*. Translated from the Russian by P. Ludwick. Moscow: Foreign Languages Publishing House, 1957.

Simmonds, George W., ed. *Soviet Leaders*. New York: Thomas Y. Crowell, 1967.

Contains biographies of the following (among others):

Dimitri Ivanovich Blokhintsev (atomic physicist), by Albert Parry.

Vladimir Alexandrovich Fock (physicist), by Siegfried Müller-Markus.

Leonid Vitalevich Kantorovich (mathematician), by Robert C. Stuart.

Pyotr Leonidovich Kapitsa (physicist), by Albert Parry.

Lev Davidovich Landau (physicist-mathematician), by Albert Parry.

Trofim Denisovich Lysenko (enemy of genetics), by Maxim W. Mikulak.

Nikolai Nikolaevich Semyonov (chemist), by Albert Parry.

Tsiolkovsky, K. E. *Selected Works*. Translated from the Russian by G. Yankovsky. Moscow: Mir Publishers, 1968.

Turkevich, John. *Soviet Men of Science: Academicians and Corresponding Members of the Academy of Sciences of the USSR*. Princeton, N. J.: D. Van Nostrand, 1963.

Vucinich, Alexander. "Nicolai Ivanovich Lobachevskii: The Man Behind the First Non-Euclidean Geometry," *Isis* 53 (1962).

Zalkind, Semyon. *Ilya Mechnikov, His Life and Work*. Translated from the Russian by X. Danko. Moscow: Foreign Languages Publishing House, 1959.

V. *Fiction*

Magidoff, Robert, ed. Russian Science Fiction: An Anthology. Translated from the Russian by Doris Johnson. New York: New York University Press, 1964.

Note: Should the reader come across the two fictionalized biographies, in English, of Dmitry Mendeleyev, by Daniel Q. Posin and Robin McKown, he may wish to know in advance that in my opinion these two books are too sugary to be good fiction; most importantly, full as they are of invented situations and imagined conversations, I do not consider them to be reliable as biographies of the great chemist.

Index